He Ain't Sh*t

A collection of stories for
women by women

Compiled by BusyB Writing

Dedication

This book is dedicated to every woman who has ever had to deal with a difficult relationship. It's okay to cry. Just don't let that pain define you.

Table of Contents

Table of Contents

I raise up my voice—not so that I can shout, but so that those without a voice can be heard…. We cannot all succeed when half of us are held back.

--*Malala Yousafzai*

Just A Little Too Sweet

C.H. Blake

He was like a fresh cup of coffee on a bad Monday morning. 6'3 chocolate skin complexion, pink lips, and a white-collar swag. Girl, brother man was *fine*—Mr. Sweet Dick as he called it. Little did I know, his "sweet" was sweeter than sugar, and his so-called "boi" was his side piece.

***

It was prom night, March 13, 2008. Me and my crew Ashlee, Tam, Rena, and Lisa all met up at the mall on the corner of 45th and 3rd.

Like always, Tam wanted to go fuck off with Rod ol' no-money-having-stay-trying-to-fuck-with-a-clean-ass-88-box-Chevy-on-26's-with-no-gas ass. Yep, *all* that. And this hoe had the nerve to fuck him in the parking lot. We waited for her to get done. You know, talking shit like always at the food court. That's when we meet Sean and Trell. Sean introduced himself and asked could he take me out, and I told him I was too young for his type. He was damn near a grown-ass man, sizing me up with that "I just wanna fuck" look in his eyes.

I'm not gon' lie... I got his number while Trell asked Ashlee if they could join us after prom. I was so gullible and naive at 18 years old, so I didn't mind the attention and late nights. Little did I know, Sean would change my life *forever*.

That following night, I remember checking my Bebo account to see who was all online. Somehow, Sean added me as a friend without knowing my last name. It was all cool because I had a feeling we would see them in the next hour or so. At that time, I wasn't thinking about what would happen if we all were smoking and doing a lot of underaged drinking.

Two hours later, we pulled up at a Motel 6 and waited on them to text us the room number. When Trell opened the door, it's like 15 old ass guys in this itty bitty room waiting as if we were coming to strip like Ronnie and Trixie off *The Players Club*. I texted Sean ASAP.

> I'm not coming in.
>
> It's too many people.
>
> You could have told us it was going to be more people.

It's cool we'll tell them to leave.

Well, he did just that. The only problem was now, these fools were drunk. So we when went in and saw the guys....let's just say me and Ashlee most definitely became friends for life after that... We all started back drinking, and somehow just wound up in the bed. Needless to say, I was nervous as hell. No way I was fucking my man in front of my best friend. At least... that's what I thought.

Ashlee undressed me, as they stood back watching. At that very moment, I knew they had added more to our drinks then they claimed. She started to kiss me, and I turned away quickly. That didn't stop her. I felt her wet lips gently kissing my neck...and the rest was history. All I'll say is that my future heartbreak was watching me from afar, his best friend standing there with his dick in his hand. At that moment, I needed to feel wanted, and they gave me just that.

After that night, Sean and I became a pair. It was nothing that this man didn't do for me. You hear me? *Nothing*. Hair done, car to drive, money... you name it, I had it.

Six months later, his true colors revealed themselves. I used to work at Dairy Queen part-time after school, and I slowly started noticing some changes. Each day, the texts dried up, voicemail always picked up, and the phone calls were short because he was too busy. It was a whole new life.

We never stayed together because he was older, and my brothers and father didn't approve of him. So, I said my piece and enjoyed him from afar like always.

At one point, I needed to confront him. I wanted answers. Why was he starting to act so different- ly all of a sudden? The minute I fixed my mouth to question him about anything, he punched me in my mouth so hard that blood started to gush from my lips. Never in my right mind did I think this dog of a so-called man would beat my ass the way he did. Not only did he whoop my ass, but he fucked me and left me in the room, taking my car keys with him. Funny thing is he forgot to get his phone. Curiously, I looked through it, and what do I see? Pictures of Trell bent over butt-ass naked with the tip of Sean's dick in him. Clearly, this was more than just a friendship. These were *lovers*, and I was tripped in the middle.

Disgusted was an understatement. I was sick, and I knew I had to tell Ashlee. So, I sent everything from his phone to mine and deleted his sent messages. While he wanted to beat on me, all I wanted was revenge. A million other thoughts went through my head. How was I to face my family like this?

I became ashamed of myself, withdrawing from everything around me. Days went by, money ran out due to paying to hide out in this room, and I couldn't take it anymore. I had to call Ashlee.

"Hey, Ashlee."
"Hey! Where have you been? Sean has been looking for you. He said he lost his phone."
"I need you to come to where I'm at. I'm gonna text you the address. Come alone, though."
"What's going on?"
"Listen. What I have to say is more important and too personal to talk about over the phone."
"I'm on my way."

About 20 minutes later, she was pulling up in the parking lot. When I opened the door, tears started to fall from my eyes.

I pulled out my phone and showed her what I saw. Talk about *hurt*. She just found out she was five weeks pregnant by Trell, and now she finds out that her man is fucking his male best friend. All this shit was crazy, but I knew the truth would set us both free. We needed to know what was going on. They had no right, jeopardizing our life for a friendly fuck.

After we both calmed down and left, I stayed over her house for a few days until I figured out how to talk to Sean and let him know that I knew the truth about his "other side."

We finally agreed to talk face to face. He started talking about how he got 9-year-old twin girls, got married young, and divorced. He wanted me to believe and understand that he always had a problem with his sexuality. Sorry, but that did *not* justify his actions.

At that point, I stopped listening. I was hurt, and all I could do was think about getting tested. When I told him that, he rammed me up against the wall. "I'll kill you before you expose me," he said in a cold voice. That night he tried. He broke my arm, cracked two of my fingers, burned my neck with his lighter, dragged me to the tub, and poured bleach down my mouth. I immediately went unconscious. All I remember was hearing Ashlee screaming, "You killed my best friend!"

When I woke up in the ICU, I was in excruciating pain, yet somehow in my heart, I loved this man. This wasn't love anymore. This was pure hate, and I felt like it was all my fault. With the help of Ashlee, Rena, and Lisa, we exposed their asses. We posted all their videos and pictures on social media and tagged them in every single one.

I gave the police the address to Sean's home...he didn't even know that I knew where he lived. He got 20 years for attempted murder and aggravated assault. Ashlee filed to get full custody of the baby, and Trell was a no show. Weeks later, we found out he was in New Orleans dressing in drag.

***

So I leave you with this: The fact that someone else loves you doesn't rescue you from the project of loving yourself. The challenge of life is to overcome. Love yourself first. You do not have to seek validation from anyone else, especially a man. Don't be like me and look for love in all the wrong places. Let it come to you naturally as you embark on your own journey to self-love.

Measure for Measure

Adriana Mucia

Unfortunately for me, most of my previous experiences with boyfriends are a load of horseshit. Fortunately for you, this one in particular is ridiculous enough to write down for your entertainment.

After graduating high school, I went to this local theater and took a two-year professional training program basically to be good enough as an entertainer to get paid for my work. It was my first day there, and I didn't know anybody. So, I decided I should at least find one person that day and get to know them.

The first class of the day was ballet, and this guy in that class caught my eye because oh no... he's hot. He's looking like a Michelangelo sculpture come to life, so let's call him Michel. No one else in the entire program could even hold a candle to Michel in beauty, and he walked around like he knew the genetic lottery he won. I decided I was gonna get him to notice me by impressing him with my ballet skills.

It was my first day dancing ever, so you can guess how well that went.

But that's fine because it's not like I had any chance with him, I thought bitterly. Even if he wasn't out of my league, any guy who's taking ballet isn't into girls anyways, right? I bet he's not even single.

Oh, how wrong I was. Single *and* into girls.

Once I found out that information, y'all, I spent—I shit you not—an entire year crushing on this dude. And he didn't even notice me any more than a normal person would notice his classmates. I day-dreamed about him, I dream-dreamed about him, I wrote about him, and I even asked his friends about him! This guy was nothing but good looks: no job, no car, no license, no insurance, no money, and no place of his own. I'm giving you this period of time to yell at this book. I know, and I wish I could build a time machine and yell at my younger self as well.

So, this went on until eventually Michel and I be-came tentative friends. His other friends started talking about how he was crushing on me, too, and how he's just trying to find the right time to ask me out.

Now, anyone with eyes and ears could see the red flags associated with his attention suddenly being on me after a year of nothing, especially after an-other girl he was talking to had just rejected his advances. But my last three brain cells thought: more for me!

So, we were officially dating, and my rose-tinted glasses were fitting me perfectly at this point.

We were together for a total of three weeks. During that time, I was stressed as all hell about him cheating on me because I wasn't putting out. I was a virgin, and I didn't feel too good having sex for the first time with someone who I'd only really known for about a month. Not to mention his years of experience with sex intimidated me, being someone who didn't have any previous encounters to learn from. We were doing other intimate stuff, don't get me wrong, and I was perfectly content with that much in such a new relationship. But he was never satisfied with me afterwards, even if he never said as much.

I was terrified of fucking up the relationship for being a "prude," without even stopping to think that maybe the guy I'm dating should care about me enough to be open and communicative about what he wants in the relationship.

Meanwhile, my family planned a trip to the Florida Keys for my mom's birthday, and I couldn't go because it was in the middle of the school week. It's important to note that I had gotten into a sizable car accident just a few days before. I already had depression, but I was in an especially bad funk because my body wasn't performing like it used to while I was healing, and I was in constant physical pain from dance classes. I decided this time, since I had the house to myself, was the perfect opportunity to invite Michel to my house and spend extra time together. You know, to make me feel better.

The day he was supposed to come home with me after class, I overheard a conversation between Michel and his best friend, Leo. This was the end of Michel's rant:

"Dude, I'm pretty much banking on smashing while I'm there because this is taking way too long."

Well, shit. Guess I have no choice but to do it, then. Obviously, I did have a choice, just to clarify to any dear readers going through something similar right now. But I didn't see it at the time because I was so hard on myself. I was trying to be the perfect girlfriend who did everything Michel wanted just to keep the relationship when I should've known that relationships aren't supposed to be that way.

I chickened out the first two days. On the third day, he was on the couch taking an afternoon nap while I was upstairs calling anyone who could give me advice. Best friends, mentors, therapist, you name it. No one picked up.

Later in the evening as we were getting ready for bed, he asked if I had condoms. I said no, because why would I have condoms if I was a virgin? So, in the ten minutes I had to myself when he went to the nearest drugstore for condoms, I called my advisors again. Again, they didn't pick up. What is going on? I had never felt more unprepared for anything.

He returned with condoms, and the short foreplay that followed did nothing to calm my nerves. But I was determined not to give him a hard time (ha) since I knew this was my chance to save the relationship. Beyond fucked up, I know.

At this point he was over me, and I could finally see that this living Michelangelo sculpture had a much bigger dick than his stone counterparts. All the phone calls in the world couldn't have prepared me for the pure agony I was put through in his attempts to fit inside me. He put me in all sorts of positions to try and get it in. All the while, my insides felt like someone shoved a hot knife in there and twisted it. After what felt like forever, I finally begged him to stop.

He went to sleep annoyed and disappointed, while I stayed up the rest of the night sore and ashamed. I had never felt more alone in my life.

After two days of Michel avoiding me in classes

and not replying to any messages, he finally had the nerve to face me in person and break up with me. I may have been pretty stupid back then, but even I knew it was because of the failed sex attempt at my house. I tried to reason with him.

"It was just the first try, we could always do it again some other time. I promise I'll get better!"
"It wasn't the sex. I'm breaking up with you because you're so sad all the time, and you act so depressed."

No shit I act depressed. I have depression! I wanted to scream at him. I was just in a car accident! I'm being overworked and no matter how hard I try I'm never good enough for the people I care about in the theater! Did you honestly think a three-week relationship with a hot guy was gonna magically fix all of that?!

Seeing through his obvious lie, but not wanting to cause a scene, I settled for being passive-aggressive around him and his closest friends whenever they tried to talk to me. This subsequently got me kicked out of the program.

***

Leaving that theater and its toxic occupants behind turned out to be the best thing that ever happened to me.

In the year that followed, I got a real degree, a real man, and the opportunity to get two more degrees on scholarship. Man, what a difference self-confidence can make!

If you take away anything from this clownery of mine, let it be this: know your worth, make sure the person you're with knows your worth, and if you have to sacrifice your identity and happiness to please the people you're with, you're with the wrong people.

Keys to Inner Power: Boundaries, Curiosity, and Self-Ownership

Heather Wylie

When my near-decade-long relationship ended, I began consuming stories. I didn't just want to read them, that wasn't enough; I needed to hear them. I began to listen to storytelling podcasts. Participants would stand on a stage in front of a crowd, naked in their vulnerability, and they would share something traumatic, funny, triumphant, or redemptive.

I listened to countless audiobooks of women overcoming assaults, domestic violence, and countless other challenges. The voices of strangers were my lifeline, keeping me afloat when I had become unanchored in my sea of grief. I needed to hear other people telling me stories so that I knew I wasn't the monster that the mean internal voice kept telling me I was.

In August of 2017, I was broken lower than I had ever been before. I used the last little bit of any money I had to buy the washer and dryer that was in my own home from my ex. I had just started a new job and was trying to build a business and was terrified that my clients would leave me because most of my friends had. I lost my religious support system, my friends, my ex's family members—and all of this loss made me realize how small my life had become. My partner had isolated me so much that I no longer had a relationship with my parents or sister.

The only friend I kept was one that I had had outside of the group of friends we cultivated. I was alone, I was in a huge financial bind, my credit score tanked, and a stranger totaled my beautiful new car outside of my house. I had nothing—no money for a down-payment and a horrible credit score— to be able to get a new one on my own. It seemed like bad thing after bad thing kept happening to me. If this was a test, I thought, I'm failing it miserably.

I felt like a person made of glass; I was so brittle that if the wind blew too forcefully, I felt like I would shatter into a million pieces in the wind. I couldn't find peace. If I was able to sleep, my dreams were trauma filled. My ex stalked me. My body, with a life of its own, often shook uncontrollably and randomly. I was depressed, anxious, and exhausted. I couldn't go into grocery stores without having a panic attack in the parking lot first. If I managed to push through that feeling, I scuttled around from aisle to aisle, praying I didn't encounter anyone because I couldn't DEAL with anyone.

My life became one of avoidance: places I didn't go to anymore because they were too hard, events that I wanted to attend but couldn't make myself get out of the car. I carried shame around me like a mantle from my relationship filled with gas-lighting and broken promises.

My character assassination in my small town through social groups started making its way back to my family. One of the most crippling challenges I faced early on was the HIPAA violation because my ex saw my doctor too, and people are too happy to spread gossip in a small town. I complained, and my medical bills mysteriously disappeared, everything swept neatly away and covered up—nothing to see here.

I had lived for years with having my voice taken from me; new narratives generated layer after layer until maybe if they were said enough, they became a new reality. Still, I remembered a vague, whispered truth of what was. Year after year, I found myself in a smaller box and smaller box. My ex chose my clothes (did that mean I liked leopard print because my ex told me I liked leopard print or did I independently like leopard print?).

I had to keep my work flexible so that I could make sure that I was home by 5:30 and could have dinner on the table by 6:00 or 6:30. I became a shell of myself. People saw a brightly colored exterior, like a doll, but my insides were grief-filled by inauthenticity.

That little voice that I had pushed down for so long started coming back. It was a real struggle because I had worked so long to silence the real me. You know, Intuition said, If he loved you, he wouldn't treat you this way. If you loved you, you wouldn't let him treat you this way. How could I show myself that I loved myself? I began to look for ways that I could keep myself safe. There were three things that I did to save myself: boundaries, curiosity, and ownership.

Boundaries were the first thing that I started to establish. Boundaries are hard. I felt like if I had boundaries, people wouldn't love me. I didn't realize that boundaries are how I tell other people how to love me. Boundaries invite change into your life: if your boundary is challenged or pressed, it lets you stand firm in your own values. Boundaries are one of the smallest ways you can start showing yourself that you have worth.

One of my best early boundaries was blocking my ex's family members from my social media and my phone. I protected myself and no longer allowed them space to send me hateful messages or use social media platforms to monitor my life. By establishing and maintaining very small boundaries,

I felt more confident in establishing and holding larger boundaries.

I knew that something had to change more than just establishing boundaries. My body had broken down. If I was mentally pushing down my experiences so I could keep moving forward, my body reminded me in physical ways that I was not okay. You are supposed to be able to sleep. You aren't supposed to shake all the time. You aren't supposed to be so tired you can't do anything. You aren't supposed to forget what you went downstairs for. Your heart isn't supposed to palpitate!

I began exploring all of the different ways that I could start to heal my body. Contact with my ex ended, and I was able to start moving forward. I had to google what "self-care" was. I kept a journal. I implemented movement (inconsistently, I hate sweating) into my routine. I made sure to establish a sleep schedule. I often used my therapist to bounce ideas off of her, and sometimes it was the same idea repeatedly. I kept approaching change with the mentality of "how" instead of one of resistance. If I tried something and it didn't work out, at least I had tried it, right?

Here's a secret: whatever I tried always made me better. Even if I wasn't able to stick to working out every day, I wasn't worse off for the two weeks that I had kept to it. Curiosity comes from the "how" mindset, and it allowed me to approach healing with a way of openness that continues to serve me nearly four years later.

***

Ownership saved me by empowering me. I struggled with this for such a long time. I thought that ownership was the same thing as shame—that if I fully acknowledged the situation, it meant I would wear my shame around like a mantle. Instead, ownership gave me power. It allowed me to step back and acknowledge the mistakes that I had made. It let me see, with compassion, things that I wished had gone differently. I was able to look at myself without judgment.

I had done bad things. I had bad things done to me. Some moments did not fill me with pride. However, there were so many more moments that did. I was able to objectively look at how I was at the beginning of my breakup and reframe how I saw myself. Before I started taking ownership of my life and decisions, I thought of that past self with shame and contempt. After I began taking ownership, I looked at her with grace. How amazing that past self was to be able to get up every morning during the hardest part of her life and keep going with the belief that maybe tomorrow would be better. The time came when there was a tomorrow that was better.

The fantastic thing about boundaries, curiosity, and ownership was that they began leaking into other parts of my life. I began thinking "what if I" and then I would do it. What if I started painting? What if I started writing? What if I rearranged my bedroom? These small changes allowed me to begin making more significant changes. What if I quit that job that made me miserable? Boundaries helped me identify what was actually okay and what wasn't, and if something wasn't okay then it had to go. I had the power to make it go. Ownership of my decisions allowed me to be in control of those changes.

I am in charge of my destiny. I am responsible for my choices. I do have power. I make things happen; things don't always happen to me. These shifts in my mindset have brought insurmountable change. I now have the ability to look at myself with compassion and begin to accept and love myself.

In the struggle of my relationship ending and mourning, a friend told me, "You are such an inspiration of resiliency! Did you know there's this desert flower that grows in the dark? That's you." You are also that desert flower, growing in the dark. You, too, have the power to start implementing change. Embrace things with a curious mind. Ask yourself "how" and "what if I" more than you allow yourself to say, "I can't." Embrace ownership because with it, you will own the choices you make, for better or worse, and you will recognize your own inherent power. Your story is your own, no one can take it from you, and you can map your future.

Mr. Unattainable

Vanessa Shevat

I fell in love with a closeted gay man. Yes, that's right. I was a silly college sophomore that fell in love with the most unattainable man in the world. Looking back, the signs were right there in front of me. In fact, they were practically screaming at me that this man was homosexual. But I was rebellious, and I didn't want to listen. So instead, I loved him with everything I had and chased after a man that would never love me back.

It all started at a restaurant in the summer of 2014. I was sitting with a friend from my college theatre troupe, and she was showing me pictures of the incoming theatre freshman boys. That's when I first saw Dimitri. I knew from that moment that I had to get to know him.

Once the school semester returned, so did the parties. I wasn't really into the party scene, but I was bombarded with invites. Truthfully, I was excited at the prospect of bumping into Dimitri, so I started going out.

One of the first parties I attended was an exclusive theatre party. Not knowing what to do, I pressed myself against the wall, watching the commotion.

One of the girls pushed a red solo cup in my hand filled with liquor of some sort. I said thank you, and wandered into the living room. That's where I saw him.

Dimitri sat on a worn-out sofa between two girls who were much prettier and skinnier than me. He had his arm wrapped around one, while the other girl sat as close as possible to him on his other side. They were both laughing at something he said, and he joined with them, running his free hand through his floppy brown hair. Dimitri was totally a ladies' man, and I was already out of the running if those were the girls he went after. Instead of approaching him, I downed my drink, and walked back into the kitchen for a refill.

Three or four drinks later, I found myself slumped against a wall in the hallway, looking into my empty cup with dismay. The party was thinning out, and only a handful of people were left. I tried to stand up to leave, but my head was spinning from the booze. I groaned and slid back down to the ground, holding my head in my hands.

"Are you okay?" I heard someone say. I opened my eyes and saw Dimitri squatting down in front of me, a worried expression on his face. Before I could answer, he pushed a cup into my hands. "It's water," he said softly.

I nodded in thanks, and took a sip, hoping he didn't notice how red my cheeks were. He watched me carefully as I finished my water and took the empty cup from my hand.

"We're gonna leave, if you wanna walk back with us," he said as he stood up. I nodded and began to stand, keeping a hand on the wall for support. "I've got you, babe," he said as he hooked his arm around my waist. He kept it there the whole walk home.

From that point on, I started to fall in love with Dimitri. I was enchanted by his presence, and I jumped at any opportunity to see him. I learned quickly that Dimitri liked to party, so I pushed myself to go with him and his group of friends (whom I didn't really get along with). I'd watch him flit between groups of girls—flirting, laughing, and drinking.

Eventually, I befriended some girls who enjoyed going out as much as Dimitri did. One night, Dimitri had agreed to walk us to a party, and as we walked along in the darkness, my friends kept telling Dimitri he should kiss me. He chuckled softly as they harassed him, and I urged them to knock it off, happy the darkness covered my burning face. Once we arrived at the party, Dimitri broke away from us as he always did.

Sometime later, after I had taken a few shots of cheap vodka, Dimitri came back. His green eyes had a playful glint in them, and he put his arm on my waist before he pulled me into a long kiss.

I thought about that kiss for days, maybe weeks after. But Dimitri never spoke about it, and neither did I.

In the months following that event, he began to accompany me to family events, and it was this unspoken assumption to everyone that we were an item. But I knew that we weren't. I noticed that he was hiding me. He would never post a picture of the both of us, he removed any tagged photos of us together, and he never told anyone about our travels or his frequent appearances at my family functions.

The first time Dimitri broke my heart was when one of my friends showed me a Snapchat story (that I had been blocked from) of him kissing another girl. After that, I confronted him. I asked what I was to him, and he said, "I'm not ready for a relationship right now." I tried to accept that, but then a few days later, in a drunken stupor, he kissed me again, leaving me even more confused and hurt.

I was so in love with him that I didn't care. I let myself believe that one day, he'd come around and admit his feelings for me. I would just wait. And I did.

I waited for years. I held my head high and waited.

Upon graduating, Dimitri landed a job on a cruise ship, so he literally sailed out of my life. I tried to forget him, but I couldn't.

In January of 2020, Dimitri reached out to me to tell me he was coming back home for two months for vacation before he sailed off again. I was wary to see him again, but let's face it... I still had feelings. So I agreed to hang out.

Covid-19 hit, and his sailing was put to a halt, extending his stay. He lived about 5 minutes away from me with his father, so it was easy to meet up. He came over often and hung out with me, my cousin Daniel, and my cousin's husband, George. During that time, I felt my love for him resurface. Then one day, in late May, I received a text from George.

"I need to talk to you about Dimitri. He's gay," he said abruptly. I felt my heart drop, and I stared at the message, confused.

Then he sent an image. On the screen in front of me was Dimitri's photo on a gay dating app. It shocked me, but I was in denial. It had to be fake.

I tried to brush it off, but one night, when Dimitri came over, I confronted him about it.

"Dimitri," I said softly. "You know you can tell me anything right?"

"Of course, babe," he said, giving me a smile. He started to walk away when I blurted it out.

"Are you gay?"

He stopped, looked at me, and hesitated. And that was answer enough for me. I felt myself crumble and go numb.

"Can we talk about this?" Dimitri asked. I nodded, and he sat down with me at the table in my cousin's house.

"How'd you find out?" he asked coldly.

Not wanting to throw George under the bus, I simply said I saw something on a dating site. Dimitri looked past me, clearly in deep thought.

"I know it was George," he said, his eyes still on something far away. He took a deep breath. "There's something else... I had sex with your cousin and George." He still couldn't meet my gaze.

That was it. That was the sucker punch I never saw coming. To say I was numb was an understatement. Dimitri being gay was one thing, but my own cousin going behind my back to sleep with him absolutely crushed my soul. Refusing to shed another tear for Dimitri, I told him to get out, and he left without any trace of remorse on his face.

I haven't contacted him since that day, and he hasn't reached out to me either. My cousin and his husband apologized to me, and against my better judgment, I forgave them.

***

I'll admit that I am utterly humiliated that I was trying to win the love of a gay man for 6 years. I wasted all that time on someone who could never love me the way that I loved him. But I don't regret it. Because of him, I know what love is.

My advice to anyone who has loved someone who didn't, or couldn't love them back is to move on. Take that heartbreak, take that rejection, and use it to build yourself up, not down.

Read This If He's Your High School Sweetheart

Abigail Mitchell

In high school, romance is something you taste. A drop of it lands in your mouth one day. Peachy, ripe—it migrates from the tip of your tongue to the more taste-bud dense sides, leaves behind its sweet aftertaste when it wanders down your throat and creeps into your bloodstream. Once it occupies a portion of your blood, you're done for.

It rushes through your veins, your heart. Your heart thrashes in response to the unknown substance. It clouds everything in a lavender haze, and the floral mist wafting through the halls seems so real you wonder if the boys have finally found a less offensive alternative to Axe body spray. Spoiler alert: they haven't.

Don't worry, it happens to everyone. Those rogue drops of romance flying around everywhere are actually respiratory droplets, I think. I mean, think about it: someone you find intriguing says, "Hello," with their chin (strong, angular jaw...) pointed in your direction, and suddenly, you can't catch your breath and your insides go pulpy. Girl, it's spiked saliva. It's the reason why kissing *feels* so intoxicating.

It happened to me freshman year. Picture this: I'm a small, pale-skinned girl wedged between childhood and adolescence. I wear too much eyeliner (*makeup goes on eyebrows, too?*), and I have a bad habit of deriving sentimentality from mundane human interactions, as well as a propensity for seeking the good in the wicked. I'm sitting in class on the first morning of the school year, and all of a sudden here comes wicked.

Looking back, I really did think he was charming. Where others saw an average kid strolling in, I saw blue eyes like crystals and a mind like a blade. He was also one of the few teenaged boys that had actually hit puberty at that point, as evident from the facial hair, which was part of the appeal.

The first time he spoke to me, I sipped that mind-altering high school romance. Just a teeny taste, and my mouth watered for more. Ben & Jerry's was less addictive than that stuff. It baffled my friends; I wanted him like an alcoholic wants to drink. I craved him more than a lioness wants to sink her teeth into a gazelle's warm and quivering hide. They asked, "Of all people, why him?" I couldn't justify my feelings, other than I thought he was smart, and intelligence is attractive to me.

"But he's not," my best friend warned. "He *thinks* he's smart, but it's an act. He's just arrogant."

I should've heeded her advice when I could, but I threw myself at him instead. The quiet, asocial girl that never got invited to anything actually had a *boyfriend*. I was on cloud nine.

As the months went by, we got closer and closer, and I felt more and more sedated by the promise of real, live romance. He was my first kiss (wet, sloppy, too much tongue), my first "I love you."

We made some memories, for sure. But memories are all that remain of that relationship.

Here's the thing—it's okay to get excited about love. It's part of life. But it's not okay to wrap up your own self-esteem in someone else's opinion of you, whether that person is your friend, your boyfriend, girlfriend, or mean girls at school.

This was my problem: I fantasize a lot. I would sit on the bus in the morning and envision the two of us together, hand-in-hand, prancing across fields and picnicking beside ponds. In my head, my boyfriend was a poetic genius. He'd write me love letters and sing in a voice that wasn't even his.

In my head, everything was doves, temperate weather, flowers, fluttering hearts... *all* that. But in reality, my "man"—who wasn't really a man yet—was walking two steps ahead of me when we went out. He wanted to play videogames when I wanted to, I don't know, talk about feelings? In reality, my "man" thought he was hot shit now because we were together. He asked for nudes and stopped talking to me for weeks when I refused. Yeah, honey. It really be like that sometimes.

And those cold daggers of intermittent silence *killed* me. What was I doing wrong? Why wouldn't he talk to me? What's wrong with me... *what'swrong-withmewhat'swrongwithme*? I'm too much, that's what. And I'm weird, and I'm annoying, and I'm ugly, and I should probably lose some weight, too. I really thought this! Because of a *guy*!

Just when that rosey, floral-scented facade of everlasting affection began to crack, he'd come and reel me in again. He wanted me when I was desperate. When I thought so little of myself and was tied up so intricately in my optimistic fantasies that I was like a flopping fish caught in a net.

In the end, it was *he* who broke it off with *me*, only to reappear several times wanting favors. I was crushed every time. Believe it or not, our break-up was the first time I really *sobbed*—shoulders heaving, screaming, and punching my poor bedroom wall like this whole thing would've never happened if it weren't for the cerulean blue paint job.

***

Years later, though, I met someone who showed me love—*true* love. It's part of the journey to love in a way that fogs your judgment, but it's not the end-all-be-all. When you're young, you don't know your worth. When you're young, love is this mystical, magical, perfect thing, and lovers can do no wrong. When you're in young love, you're intoxicated by could-be's and should-be's, but the truth is, none of it's real. The scent of his cologne (or her perfume) puffs through your nostrils on the school bus, and your pupils dilate at thoughts of them. But if they're not the one, they're just not the one. And no illusion of mutual care can change that.

True love goes deeper. It doesn't creep through the air like an apparition of daydreams and desires. It isn't the mist of infatuation spraying from the mouths of high school sweethearts. It's as real as an organ pulsing in your belly and breathing like a lung. You'll know when you find it.

If you ever find yourself in a situation like mine, where you want your lover to be something other than what they already are (and really feel like they *could* be if they just did x, y, and z), stop right there. If you're in a relationship characterized by the highs of idealism and the lows of self-loathing, facilitated by hope and manipulation, know that

that isn't what true love is like. Trying to pretend it is will only make things worse.

Real, honest love is out there. The man or woman of your dreams does exist, but not in the way you envision on the bus ride to school or the commute to the office. And when you find them, you'll wonder why you ever put up with the b.s. your exes put you through. When you find them, it won't be perfect, but it'll be something both of you value, and both of you work at naturally. It'll raise your self-esteem, not lower it. It'll ground you to reality instead of flinging you up into phantasmic clouds. It'll show you a reality that is tender and beautiful and staunch.

So, if you find yourself sobbing into your pillows at night, punching walls, and generally going crazy over a guy who keeps giving you the silent treatment and then asking for nudes, I'm telling you, honey, he ain't sh*t.

The Perfect Marine

Lorain Rizk

When I first saw Steve, my brain went, "Wow." He was the type of guy anyone turned around to look at when he entered the room. He was tall, handsome, and had a way of carrying himself as if he *knew* he was wanted. I entered the building of my last job for the first time, a local gym not too far from my house. It was the day of my interview, and I was excited to learn more about a position available in my field of study.

The general manager I had spoken to on the phone, Wesley, called me over from the reception area and had me follow him by his desk to interview him. Two desks over, the most handsome man I had ever seen was sitting right there. Throughout the entire interview process, I couldn't take my eyes off of him. *He must be an employee here*, I thought.

After Wesley brought me around for a tour of the gym, we went back to his desk, and he said, "I think you're a great fit for this position. I would like to introduce you to our Vice President, Steve."

Imagine my surprise when Wesley walked over to the man I wasn't able to stop staring at for the past twenty minutes. My heart instantly started racing.

This gorgeous man, Steve, was the Vice President of the company that I was trying to work for. He sat right across the desk from me and went on in detail about the position, salary, commissions, and bonuses. To this day, I can barely remember what he said during that five-minute meeting I had with him, but I can still remember in exact details what he was wearing and the way his deep blue eyes made me feel.

Two days later, Wesley called me to tell me I got the position. I was happy, of course, but all I could think about was the day I was going to see my new Vice President again. A few days went by after starting to work there, and there he was. I knew nothing about that man besides the fact that he was going to be my boss, but damn if he was handsome and very well-spoken. Somehow, he always knew the right things to say, and he had this way of having anyone he spoke to fall in love with him.

Steve spent a lot of time training me—evidently, much more than my co-workers. Other employees would express that there was a sense of favoritism. They told me he didn't usually spend as much time training the others as he did with me. I had never been in a situation where I felt so attracted by my boss, and one thing I was firm on was that I wasn't going to risk *my* job for a *man*.

At that time, I didn't even consider taking a step to

making that happen. Plus, he had mentioned a few things about his personal life that were red flags for me. He told me he was married but his relationship with his wife wasn't the best; he left her in Buffalo to seek his new position as a Vice President. Also, his many years spent in the Marines made me feel he may not have been a stable person, even if he looked like a perfect one.

A few weeks went by, and one day while we were working, Steve and I had a moment that made me realize he felt the same way about me as I did for him. We looked into each other's eyes for five seconds or so; that's when I knew I was in trouble. The following day, he asked me if I wanted to join a work dinner with some other employees from our company. I knew what he was doing when I realized I was the only one—other than Wesley—to be invited. I decided to go. He was my Vice President after all, and I still had to do my part at having him on my side.

Prior to leaving my house for dinner that night, he texted me the restaurant's address, and he started an irrelevant conversation with me that no boss would ever do. I felt special and honored. Even though I knew it was wrong, I couldn't help thinking about him in a different way as well. He was impossible to avoid. When I arrived at the restaurant, a couple of other employees from other locations joined that I didn't know yet. It was clear to me an hour later that something went down between him and another employee, Jessica. She wasn't pleased about the fact that I was there and how well Steve and I were getting along. I mean, it was like no one else was at the table. We were focused on each other, and everyone could see it.

After dinner, we were all pretty tipsy. Steve invited everyone back to his place, but only me, Wesley, and his date joined. Jessica didn't come, and I later found out she was butt hurt I was going. On the way to our cars from the restaurant, Wesley warned me, "He and Jessica have something going on. If you want a friendly suggestion, don't mess with him. Remember, he is still your boss."

At Wesley's words, I believed him, but I wasn't ready to give up on the idea of what could have happened between us. He was a real catch.

Once we arrived at Steve's place, all of us got really high on weed. I found it strange a boss would smoke with his employees but whatever.

"I always have weed around," he said. "It helps with my PTSD."

Not even the word 'PTSD' scared me away. After Wesley and his date left, it was only Steve and I. We sat on the couch and talked about our past trips and things we had in common. I still couldn't believe I was sitting right there, with him, on his couch in his apartment.

"You drank and smoked. Are you sure you can drive? You can stay here if you want," he said.

"I'm fine. I'm able to drive home. Thank you anyway."

We got up from the couch and walked toward the door. I turned the knob and before making my way out, we kissed. That kiss was the beginning of my troubles. We got instantly addicted to each other and a week later I found out Jessica was pregnant with his twins; eventually, she had an abortion. After convincing me I was the love of his life, I gave myself to him completely, but I always felt there were things about him I didn't know and were unclear about.

A month later he proposed to me, moved into my apartment, and lost his job a week later because of our relationship. He started to become mentally and physically abusive. Finally, one day, after a few weeks of depression and aggravated PTSD, he took all of his belongings while I was at work and left me a letter telling me he needed time alone. Four months later, I found out he went back to Buffalo to his wife, and a year later, their baby girl was born.

***

Since the day he left, I never saw him again. When I knew he was in Buffalo, I texted him to tell him how disgusted I was by what he did. All he could say was, "Things happen, and maybe one day, you'll understand."

I never understood how someone can ask to marry you a month earlier, make you feel like the love of his life, and then abandon you with a letter to never come back. I never blamed myself for what happened; it was obvious to me he had major issues. At first, I felt like I would've never found the same connection as I had with him. I thought I would have never gotten over him. But I did. I focused on my job and exercising; that was my way to become better and forget about the past.

It has been over two years now, and I still wonder how his life is today and why he did what he did, but I will never find these answers inside of me. One thing I know is that today I am happy with my life. I am happily married, and I have a beautiful daughter, who is my whole life. Real love will come knocking at your door one day, but God will test you first to make sure you are strong enough. Be patient, ladies, your time is coming.

Not Another Military Wife

Devynn E. Craig

At eighteen, I had already been through a huge heartbreak. The last thing I needed was to be flirted with by a crazy kid hanging on the side of my friends' truck at a bonfire that I didn't even want to go to. Who is this kid?

My question was answered by a follow request on Instagram and a DM inviting me to the lake later that week. I still didn't even know who he was or what he looked like, but a friend wanted me to go with him, so I did. That same crazy ass kid who hung off a truck going forty miles an hour, broke my beer bottle in my hand trying to flirt with me. I guess I fell for it because he could make me laugh, and that was a quality I loved in a person.

We started dating and went through a lot within the first three months, like A LOT. He was already enlisted in the military by the time we got together, and he was about to leave when he turned eighteen. Yeah, he was a year younger than me and people loved to remind me. He left for boot camp after we had been dating for three months. The long-distance thing worked, at least I thought it did, but it was extremely hard. I developed insomnia like crazy, staying up until 4 a.m. watching Netflix, waiting by my phone for calls, and waiting by the mailbox for letters. We just made it work.

After boot camp came training. In the midst of training, we got married. I agreed to marry him, completely ignoring the fact that he'd lied to me during his training about partying and God knows what else. Yes, after only six months of dating. I know what you're thinking—I'm an idiot, I know. What can I say? I was young, dumb, and well, you know the rest! Go ahead and roll your eyes now because I guarantee it gets worse.

The first year of our marriage was pretty normal. We got to move in together when he was stationed at his first command, we got some animals, and everything seemed dandy. We didn't know much about each other's lives before our lives together, but that didn't seem to matter. We loved each other, and we made it work.

I had always wanted to wait until I was around the age of twenty-five to have a baby, but he *wanted* a baby. After trying for almost a year, it finally happened.

I was pregnant and it was the happiest and scariest moment of my life. I was terrified of what our families would think, but it didn't matter.

I had our daughter at age twenty. I was so excited to be a mom; it's something I have wanted my whole life. Within the first few days of being home, I quickly realized that I would be doing everything by myself. I wasn't able to take a shower without putting my baby in her seat in the doorway, which meant that I had to cut my shower to five minutes or less each time. You all know that it takes more than five minutes to do anything in the freaking shower! My legs were neglected, and I felt like a damn Chewbacca.

Since I breastfed, Tyler thought that there was nothing he could "help" with. As if I didn't need to eat, the baby didn't need a diaper change, or bath, or someone to just hold her so that I could go to the freaking bathroom, right? Guess not.

Within the first two months of my baby's life, Tyler had to go on multiple detachments. In the military, those are like mini deployments, or work trips, in more basic terms. During these detachments, I would usually go to visit my family who lived a few hours away, and sometimes I'd bring my best friend with me whose husband was also in the military.

The next detachment came at the beginning of October, so naturally, my friend and I went to visit my mom. She thought it would be fun to have an early Halloween party. Now, my friend's husband worked with my husband, so he was also on this detachment with him.

The first night at my mom's house, my best friend got a call from her husband. She looked defeated when she hung up the phone.

"I need to talk to you about something," she told me.

My heart literally dropped into the deep pit of my stomach, and I instantly knew what it was. "What happened?!"

"Kaden said that he just saw Tyler leave with Brianna to her hotel room. He told me not to tell you until he knew all of the details, but I just couldn't wait to tell you. You deserve to know."

I burst into tears at that point. I didn't know what to do or what to think. I'm sitting there with my two-month-old baby in my arms, bawling my eyes out. On first instinct, I grab my phone to call him. I called over and over again, but he wouldn't answer any of my calls. So, I had to resort to texting, which I hated.

What the fuck, Tyler! You went to her fucking room with her?! And cheated on me? How could you?!

```
I was only walking her
back to her room because
she was wasted, and she
needed help.
```

```
            I didn't cheat on you,
            but I want a divorce.
```

This has to be a damn joke, right?! There's no way in hell that my husband could be cheating on me or wanting a divorce is there?

At this point, I'm fuming and ready to break something or *someone*. I run into my mom's room, and all it takes is me coming through the door for her to know what was up.

"No, he didn't!"
"He did."

My mom always has my back. She's ready to throw down at this point with whoever crosses her. She just hugs me as I sit there and bawl my eyes out. Meanwhile, I hear my best friend screaming in the background. I run back to my room and sit with her. She hangs up the phone and explains that her husband just called her screaming because she told me after he said not to, and now everything is messed up. He's pissed because he wasn't able to get all of the details before I blew up on Tyler. She's upset for me *and* because her husband just went off on her. As for me, I sit there having no clue what the hell is going to happen to my life.

I wait until the next day to text him since he wouldn't answer my call.

> I'm willing to forgive and forget. Please don't break up our family. I'm begging you.

No. I'm sorry, I still want a divorce. And I think it's best if you move out.

So, there I was. Alone with a two-month-old baby. No house to live in, no husband, nothing. My mom, of course, took me in and helped out with everything, so I was never scared of being on the streets. I went back to work and supported my baby. I was in a bad depression for a few months, I lost a bunch of weight (not a healthy amount), and felt lost and alone for a while.

During the next few months as I'm trying to move on, I find out even more shit! He would take off his wedding ring before work, he'd bring this girl to my house, he told her he loved her and he wanted her to meet our daughter, etc. He started dating the girl he left me for, knocked her up, and then they didn't even work out. Unbelievable, right? I know.

***

After around seven months after the split, I started dating again. Then he had the balls to come back and say, "I want another chance." Sorry, but now that I found my self-worth, I'm never going back. It took a lot of strength for me to do that, but I was finally in a good place for myself, and I was loving the person I was becoming.

I truly wish him the best, and I will always care for him as the father of my child. I hope he truly finds the one that makes him happy and makes him a better man. He isn't a bad person for doing this, and he doesn't deserve any bad karma. People grow and learn from their mistakes as I know he has. All I know is we just simply weren't meant for each other.

It took a lot for me to move past this heartbreak; it did. I'm not here to cherry coat the process. It's tedious and extremely hard, but YOU CAN DO IT! Keep your family and friends close to you, they are your biggest support system. I know it's hard, and I know you feel like you'll never overcome this. Those feelings are all just temporary. You are brave, beautiful, and extremely worth it.

It Be The Church Guys...

J.R. Smith

I didn't know what to feel or how to feel—he was the first guy I had ever fallen for or felt *those* types of emotions for. He made me all warm on the inside and giggle like a little girl. We met randomly on campus my freshman year and started kicking it. He was sweet, charming, and it appeared he only had eyes for me.

We had kissed a few times during the talking stage but nothing more. I wanted to be sure about him before we took that next step. One night, he and I had a long conversation about our lives and where we saw this relationship going. It was an extremely long conversation, him telling me his dreams and aspirations, and me, being the dumbass I was, nodding and not saying anything. Once he was done with his spill, he looked at me, his eyes wondering where I stood.

For the first time in my life, I was speechless.

He told me that he really liked me and wanted to be in a relationship with me. That's what I wanted also, but I couldn't bring myself to say that. I smiled at him and told him that I wasn't looking for a relationship, and I was wanting to have fun.

To this day, I understood why I said it, but at that moment in time, my mouth said something that my heart didn't feel.

So ironically, we drifted apart. We didn't hang out as often as we used to, but we were still very cordial, texting/calling each other late at night and checking in.

Moving into my first semester of my sophomore year, I noticed that this young freshman was giving me the side-eye and talking shit on Twitter. She would call him her 'Sunshine' and all this other shit, which I knew was his nickname. (Oh, for the sake of this story, we'll call ol' boy 'Chaz'). Me not knowing any better, I called Chaz and asked him what was up with ol' girl. I wasn't upset or jealous or anything, I just wanted to know why this young girl was trying to pick a fight with me.

Of course, Chaz told me not to worry about her, she's just a friend. I let it go and went about my business, but the girl was still present in my life because my so-called friends were friends with her and we all hung out together. So this shit went on through Halloween, with ol' girl approaching me wanting to fight over him.

Me? Fight over a nigga? I think the fuck not!

I casually laughed in the girl's face and walked off,

mad as hell. Once I was away from the crowd, I pulled out my cellphone and called Chaz, cussing him out from A to Z. (This is a big deal because he didn't cuss and didn't like cussing at all). He apologized on the phone, and we disconnected.

A few days later, I noticed ol' girl was avoiding me. When I came to sit with my friends, she would get up and leave. I didn't think anything of it until I checked her social media and saw all pictures of them gone. So I guess they were dating, and he broke it off with her. I chuckled to myself because it was funny how I had some type of power in his life still.

The second semester of my sophomore year rolled around, and I get a Facebook friend request from some random girl. I accepted her friend request and kept it moving—I didn't know who she was, but she was from my area, so I assumed she knew me from mutual friends. It was a late school night, and I went to the library to finish some work. When I walked in, I saw Chaz and the girl who friend requested me all chummy in a corner together. Now keep in mind, Chaz and I were still talking almost every day, so I'm furious! But I always keep a calm face and approached the two of them.

She looked at me crazily, and I looked at him with my makeshift smile, asking him about our classwork and what homework we needed to complete.

I bullshitted the conversation for about 20 minutes and then stopped mid-sentence, looked at ol' girl, and asked who she was.

She politely said that she was his girlfriend. My eyes lit up (not sure if it was out of anger or disbelief), and then I apologized for interrupting them and left the library.

Later that night, Chaz called me, upset with *me* for being so rude. The nerve of him, right? I told him to never speak to me again and hung up the phone. That should have been a huge red flag to me, but I'm still Lieutenant Dumbass.

The summer approached, and here comes Chaz again, wanting us to rekindle our friendship. I asked him about his girlfriend, and he said that they had broken up because he wanted to be with me and only me. Like an idiot, I believed his lie, and we began talking again, this time us becoming more intimate.

I'm not going to lie, I had fun fucking him, and we *definitely* enjoyed each other's company. I was starting to believe I was his girlfriend because he was treating me like I was. My first semester of my junior year was amazing, and I thought I knew what love was.

But here comes social media being the bitch that she is.

I saw that he was tagged in a picture with some other woman, and I confronted him about the picture. Chaz told me that she was a church friend, and they were on a church retreat in the picture. I believed him because the story was very plausible; he spent a lot of time with his church family and did a lot of community work with them.

That was the first and last picture I saw of them together on social media.

Christmas time came, and I was anxious because this would have been the first time a man was going to buy me something for Christmas. He and I spent our entire Christmas break together every day, all day with no interruptions. On Christmas Eve, he asked if I would pick him up and take him to the mall. I greedily said yes, thinking that he was picking out my gift. We spent all day in the mall, and he made no notion of buying anything. I didn't think too much of it...we were going to spend Christmas day together.

Christmas day came, and I got no phone call from him. I texted him with no response. I was pretty upset about it and sent him a nasty text, demanding that he answer the phone. Again, no response from him. Later that night, as I was lying in bed, I scrolled on Facebook and saw a picture I will never forget....

Remember the girl I had asked him about previously, and he lied and said that was his church friend? Well, lo and behold, he proposed to her on Christmas. All of his friends and family were tagging him in a post, congratulating the two of them.

I didn't know how to feel. I had forgotten how to breathe. Anger wasn't my first emotion; I had a bag of mixed emotions. I kept to myself the rest of Christmas break until I returned to classes in January.

As soon as I stepped foot on campus, all eyes were on me. The college I graduated from was very small, and everyone knew everything about each other. There was a lot of hushed conversations around me, and all of my friends were hesitant to speak to me.

One friend, in particular, came up to me and gave me a hug, telling me that it was okay to cry, but I refused to. I refused to have anyone see me break. I was too strong for that shit.

I kept my composure for the first 3 weeks—on that 4th week, I abruptly left class one day and ran to the restroom. The same friend who hugged me followed me to the bathroom to find me sobbing loudly in the bathroom stall.

I was broken, and Chaz was the reason why I was broken. I was angry. I was hurt. I was fucking furious. I wanted to clock that nigga in the face...and at that moment, I began to realize that niggas ain't shit.

I was sad, and my sadness was apparent to everyone I encountered. My friends tried to cheer me up, but nothing was working. I knew I would be better if I was able to whoop Chaz's ass, but ironically, he was missing in action.

***

What I learned from this is that loyalty and honesty are hard to come by these days. To the woman that's reading this, understand that a man who wants you will not leave you questioning where you stand—he will be straightforward in his pursuit of you. Never chase a man, let a man chase you. If there's any doubt in your gut, trust your instincts and leave that man alone.

The Poet Panty Dropper

Savvy Rose

All the girls in my high-school went after the sporty, meat-head, adonis types. The more popular the better.

Not me. I was drawn to the "pimped-out-whips" with loud bass and smooth candy paint that covered the sleek bodies of fast sports cars. The more modifications the better, and in my small town, there was a local hang-out in the back of a Wendy's parking lot. This was where all the drag racing happened and the boys with slicked-back hair could show off their booming sound systems. I know, classy, right?

I should also mention, this was at the time when the movie Fast and the Furious first came out, and everyone wanted to be like Paul Walker, with his impeccable racing skills and giant set of balls. And let's not forget to mention, having a hot chick on your arm or sitting on the hood of your car, just like Eva Mendes and Gal Gadot.

Who wouldn't want to be like those sinewy, push-up-bra clad racer chicks? I sure did. When you're a 17-year-old senior in high school, only in your wildest dreams would you be able to look like one of those perfectly shaped broads with the long mermaid hair and greased-up long legs.

So, there I sat in a parking lot, in the passenger seat of a shiny Toyota Celica, bass booming around me and the night's dark skies mixing with the various neon lights. That's when I saw him. Casanova in the flesh.

He always had a girl in the passenger seat of his black on black "whip". This is probably what sticks out to me the most, and possibly why he was so interesting to me: completely unattainable. I don't really mean that he was always in a committed relationship, it was more like he had a waiting line, and trust me, that line was fairly long. He was tall, handsome, and fit. What I remember the most was how his hazel eyes seemed to penetrate me. That was me—always looking for a deep meaning in everything. I was very obsessed with the idea of a soul mate, someone who could love you for all your flaws and even make you a better version of yourself. Hell, I still believe that today, I won't lie. Perhaps, that is why I write Fantasy Fiction.

Casanova had a smile that could make just about any girl blush. It was a crooked, devilish smile that he would give me every time we would pass each other in the hallways. I was slightly attractive but also extremely shy, and I never spoke to him at all.

That is until later, long after high school and after lots of self-discovery. By now I was close to mid-twenties and had a child of my own. I was in a very unfulfilling and one-sided relationship and Facebook was the new MySpace. Casanova's face popped up in my 'People You May Know' bar, and after a few too many glasses of wine, I hit 'Request.' It wasn't long before we were chatting via Facebook and other social platforms.

It was so exciting when he came back with a message that said, "I've always liked you, I always thought you were hot." My excitement at this absolutely bubbled over, and I was quickly wrapped up in high school memories.

The first time I read his work was online. Back in high school, I had no idea this handsome fellow also had an affinity with words. Once I delved deep into his art, it wasn't long before the poetry had me descending into a self-procured fantasy of pure lust. I loved words, and I still do. If a guy knew how to talk and made words sound like candy-coated hearts, I was quickly head over heels—talk about my perfect panty-dropper.

Casanova always wanted to meet on the down-low. I mean, I did too. There were stolen kisses and flirtations at a couple of small-town bars. There was even a salacious encounter in a driveway that involved a middle-of-the-night meet up and our two bodies under the stars. Yeah, that was a spectacularly vivid night that I will always remember. He was always whispering into my ear and making romantic declarations via text.

While I was at home, reading his two-liner poetry, thinking they were about me, he was taking photos of his girlfriends and traveling. I was just a side piece, but a willing side-piece. Who knew how many women he had held inside his DMs and Facebook Messenger? Countless, I'm sure. I would look through his followers and who he followed with a sick feeling in my stomach. There were hundreds of make-up covered, half-dressed women, inhabiting all the classic selfie poses and clichés.

The girlfriends came and went, but I was never a contender. Never chosen for the girlfriend job, always just an after-thought in the background, a drunken sext.

My value slowly decreased right along with his empty words. All designed to suck you in, only they spit me back out. I took his poetry to heart and saw myself within them. I based my value on his words and actions. His piercing eyes, his seductive smile, all left me feeling worthless each dawning of every morning. This poetry fantasy world that I entered into each night, usually drunk on wine, was always followed by a literal and figurative hangover. The next day, my pounding head would recall the exchange of scathing words. Undoubtedly followed by the sobering realization that I meant nothing to him.

***

It took months of this back and forth for me to realize that he wasn't going to save me from my unhappy arrangement. I had to do that. I had to find the courage in myself to become independent and take care of myself and my child all on my own, sweet nothings not needed. I left that man who had me in that unfulfilling relationship, and I also left Cassanova behind as well.

In the end, I needed to learn a very hard lesson about validation. I don't need an attractive, smooth-talking man to validate my appearance, my worth, or my status. That is my job. Maybe I just liked the words, and words were anybody's property. We can all speak and write words. So now, my passion is words and writing. I pour my fantasies and my desires into my characters, and I hone my craft each and every day. Maybe it wasn't a love affair with Cassanova, but just a love affair with beautiful and poetic verses.

Co-deep-in-it

Leya Greene

To whoever needs to see this: romance material only serves as a blueprint on what NOT to do.

I was always a late bloomer: didn't get my first phone until I turned 13, didn't lose my virginity until I turned 19, didn't get my license until I turned 21. But I wasn't always so innocent; got my first kiss at 9, smoked weed for the first time at 14, crashed my first car at 17.

That's what happens, growing up with daddy-issues; certain things just end up happening backwards. Instead of learning to defend, I learned to comply. Instead of learning to speak up, I learned to obey. Instead of learning to have fun, I learned to skate by. Instead of learning to love, I learned to fuck. The problem was, again, I was a late bloomer. I only wanted to fuck for love so when the time came (ha), I couldn't for the life of me tell the difference.

I gave my virginity to my high school crush. Cute, right? Nope. I fell for a chubby, white, minute-man-child, notoriously known for being the biggest fuck-boi in school. He broke my best friend's heart, and three years later his car was in my port (ha ha). I broke my first love's heart just days before. In my opinion, my following experiences were just karma's way of saying, "How do YOU like it, hoe?"

I felt like it was the universe punishing me. I felt no remorse for the sorry jock-strap I had lead on for a month (I still don't. He was a bitch), but I knew I had a lot of growing up to do when I met Montreal. Now, this was back in my, "fuck these niggas" stage, where I ended up joining a gaming chatroom for an underground rapper I was fond of (Surprise! ALSO a bitch). I met some friendly people, almost got too friendly with some, and got entirely too comfortable with others. I was the source of a lot of drama, I'd like to think, mainly because they still ask about me (*petty intensifies*).

Montreal was the only good thing to come out of that whole ordeal. My dumbass, as a lonely, naive 20-year-old, spent thousands of dollars flying myself out to actually spend time with these dry fucks (*lmao* I can't stand me right now). The first, Dade, couldn't give two shits if he held 'em in his bare hands. Here's how fucking crazy I was: after comforting him through a family death, attempting to talk him down from suicide, and staying on my best behavior after breaking things off for both our sakes, I have yet to take him to court for leaking my sex-tape (this was the first, but not the last); but my petty ass sure was satisfied after he felt the need to send me death threats just because I had a sweet little conversation with his girlfriend about what he'd been up to for the past year. Why the hell should I keep his secrets when he couldn't even be trusted with the püm?

Things didn't get better with the second, Jackson. After whiskey-dick, a salmon dinner, and silence, that cuck couldn't even muster up a side-eye before my departure. He knew Dade so well that he was man enough to pretend he didn't know about the leak at all (everyone knew, even their little cult-leader). Both have attempted to make amends, but women like me do not respect liars or cowards. Jackson has actually killed people, and even HE couldn't look me in the eye.

Montreal was another story. We got comfortable, sure, but it wasn't just talking game. For hours, we'd take up each other's time, just because neither of us wanted to be alone. He'd go do his thing, and I'd sit there, waiting for the next call. Yikes, unhealthy much? I thought so, too. He seemed to be the only person who saw past what I could potentially "give" him, and as a result, got a sneak-peak of my inner turmoil. I spent a year praying he'd be mine, but that ship sailed almost a decade ago. I couldn't cope; he had all these things he was working toward and all my time was spent... consumed... by the thought of him.

I was in way too deep. To make matters worse, he offered to cover the rest of my plane ticket just so we could meet sooner. I mean, C'MON. I went out of my way to warn him; I KNEW this shit was not going to end well. I felt like a teenager again, writing dates on the airport bathroom walls and shit. Love-making, conversing, intimate showers, dancing in the kitchen, old movies, and even older music: I fell HARD. So hard, in fact, I cried all the way home, and he was on the phone with me the entire time.

Several mental breakdowns and a 'goodbye' voicemail later, and we go from talking every single day to silence. Two years of pretending I don't care, despite the fact I'm still checking his social media, just to see if he thinks of me every now and again. I had some serious soul-searching to do, and I couldn't keep chasing unrequited love. It was painful, exhausting, and time consuming. I watched a video where a woman spoke on her own journey of self-love and acceptance. She spoke of isolation; said it would be painful, lonely, and mentally unbearable, but absolutely necessary, even vital.

So that's what I did.

It's what I do best- disappearing without a trace for unforeseeable spans of time. That's depression, such shameful emotional storms just gave me more of a reason to suffer alone. Other than the occasional fling, I ceased to take relationships, and sex, seriously at all. I never really understood the separation of love and sex until I had my first threesome, age 22. I remembered witnessing an incredibly intense climax in third person, and in that moment I developed a new-found respect for sex, both with and without connection. With no strings attached, I was able to come (okay, okay, I'll stop) to terms with my physical body, finding comfort in my flesh, and removing my insecurities, replacing them with internal pleasures. With a connection that goes deeper than sex, I found a new language to help express the feelings I can't verbally convey.

But, what is there to express when no one's listening? I grew up thinking people found little use for me. My words, my thoughts, my feelings; these were always neglected. So, of COURSE, I'm acting a whole fool the first time anyone shows even the slightest interest in me at all. That wasn't love, and I think my heart already knew that, but I could never let Montreal go, even when it felt like he was absent when he was with me.

On my last day with him, I remember praying (to whoever would listen) for us to always find each other; that no matter how far, no matter the circumstance, that we'd never part, whether I got to be his lover or not. At that point, it didn't matter if we were able to be friends or not... I just didn't want to live without him.

***

It's been a month since I started talking to him again. My god, people can really grow in two years. On my end, I found love as soon as I stopped looking for it. It sounds incredibly cliché, but it's true. I remembered some online advice I found when it came to determining if one was truly in love: if, after six months, the "wow-factor" hasn't worn off; if, after 12 months, there's still so much to learn about each other; if, after 18 months, the feelings of compassion and tenderness still linger; if, after two years, the couple can still find reasons to laugh, then the chances of this love developing into a healthy, long-lasting relationship is increasingly more likely.

In Montreal's case, he's grown in different ways, too, mostly internal. He was the perfect shoulder to cry on, but it never felt like he really gave a fuck just because he was physically present. What surprised me this time around was his willingness to speak. It felt like he built a window right into the wall he built around himself, just so he could wave to me every once in a while. He revealed to me how hard it was for him to finally open up, and that the possibility of losing me forever really made him think about the price of his own silence. I guess this was karma's way of letting me know: lesson learned.

I'd like to think my prayers were answered, but

I can't speak so soon. All I know is this: my faith in myself is completely justified. I always try my best to give others the same love I wish I had, and I think in doing so, I helped him realize there's more to love than just what can be given; receiving is strangely difficult when all anyone ever does is take back what they've given away. I think that, in only asking for Montreal's companionship, I asked him to release his demons, at least enough to embrace me.

There's a certain freedom in vulnerability: when you can finally stop pretending you aren't suffering, when someone is there to cry with you, when someone finally allows themselves to cry.

Moral of the story: get you a man who cries.

My Favorite Liar

Sammy K.

Kendrick. Effin' Kendrick. He was a top dog, hall of famer, type of football player. The type that could just smile and make your panties soaking wet. I'm talking make you lose your train of thought just by walking by kind of jock. Was it the way that he made me laugh that made me feel like I was on cloud 9 every time I heard his name? Or was it the way he fucked me that had me ready to risk it all to get some more of his love again? Ladies, come get this tea.

As you probably guessed, I was in college. My roommate went over to her new boyfriend's room, and there was Kendrick—sitting around talking shit with his guys, looking like a fresh box of Imma fuck that pussy up. As soon as I walked into the room, he looked up at me and gave me this big sexy smirk.

"Dang, you cute!" he said with slight grin forming across his lips. I giggled. I'm just a little socially awkward, so I didn't really know how else to respond. On top of that, I just got out of a seven-year relationship, so I wasn't really feeling all that attractive. Truthfully, I just thought he was another guy trying to get into my pants or whatever. Now, don't get me wrong, I definitely thought Kendrick was cute too, but that was all. I didn't really think much of it at the time.

A few days go by, and I hear a knock. Guess who was standing there looking back at me with those big brown eyes? *What the hell is he doing here?* I thought to myself. *He must be at the wrong door.*

"Hey, you're that girl from the other day, right?" he asked.

"Yeah," I said softly.

"Hey, you cute," he said, repeating himself from a few days ago. "We're going to go to a party later, and I wanted to invite you." Oh really?

"Okay, cool. I'll catch you there," I said as I closed the door. Since I was going to be seeing Kendrick there, I decided that I needed to put a little extra effort into my outfit. Instead of the usual jeans and t-shirt, I was going to get *fine* and *fancy* and wear tight shorts (not to be confused with coochie cutters), a halter top, and some jewelry. Yes, this was fancy for me. The sexiest tomboy you'll ever see. *wink*

So, I show up at the party and see Kendrick... drunk. Not completely sloppy but pretty dang close. He sees me and walks up to me with that grin of his.

"You are just *so* fine," he gushes with slurred words. "You're going to come home with me." I know he's drunk, so in my mind, I knew I wasn't trying to go there with him. Well...let's just say fate had other plans for me. After about seven beers and one too many shots, I was drunk as a skunk too. So... I ended up at his house.

It was on this day that I found out what an anaconda was, and ladies...it changed my *whole freaking* life. I was smitten. I was high as hell off of anything and I mean *anything* he did or said.

This man could simply *walk* into the caf at school. I wouldn't even be looking at him, and my whole face would turn red. I would just *know* he was in there. How crazy is that? Just the thought of his presence had me blushing. Or he would text me with something random. He lived off-campus, right, so the conversation would look something like this:

```
Hey wyd

                          Nothing. Wassup?

I'm on campus. Can you
come see me?
```

Ladies...I shit you not...before I even sent the message, my ass was already on the other side of campus trying to find him. He would hit me with another text like this:

```
Hey, I'm hungry. Do
you have anything to eat?
```

How do I respond? I'm trying to buy him food or whip something up real quick so he can eat. I was Superman and had come face to face with my kryptonite. This man had me practically floating every single day. If I was available, I was his. If I wasn't available, I would count down the seconds til I was so I could be around him again. I'm literally in class not paying attention because I'm thinking about when's the next time I'm gonna get some. It was that. Damn. Good.

I had no shame. But of course, every high has to come down at some point. So, Kendrick was at the dorms a lot because he didn't have any internet at home. What he would do is either go to the library to get his work done or he would come to my room so we could hang out afterward. One day he left his laptop, so he got a hold of mine and put his email address on there. I minimized the screen so he wouldn't have to log out, thinking that I would just let his email sit there on my computer untouched. I'm shaking my head as I write this because he had no idea that he was dealing with Miss Inspector Gadget, the female FBI.

What does Sammy do? Oh nothing, she (and by she I mean me) just went through every single Facebook message he had. I'm talking time stamps and all because I am efficient in my investigations (flips hair). Come to find out, some of the times he was supposed to come hang out with me, he was hanging out with a bunch of other chicks.

Me being me, I asked him about it. He always said, "What are you talking about? No, no, I would never do something like that." Sigh. It was that same stereotypical shit you see in the movies.

He would hit me with the, "Hey, can you come over?"
Then, I would be like, "Yeah, I'll come over."
We do our thing and all of a sudden, he's like, "I got somewhere to go."
But *why*, though. (-_-)

Yeah, that kind of stuff started happening. But the funny thing about it is that I completely pushed past it. I literally ignored all his lies because he was never rude. He was never hateful. He always made me laugh, and he kept a smile on my face. He was just a *good* damn liar.

We were three years into our talking stage, and I was never his girlfriend. Three damn years. He claimed he wanted me to be his girlfriend, but he never could let his ex go.

One day, I had to finally let him know what was what. He invited me over. We had a long conversation because I was finally single. Like, single to the point that I was 100% over my ex and ready to be Kendrick's wife.

"Sooo..." I started. "When can we actually be together?"
"Right now...it's just not good timing."

As soon as I heard that, something clicked. A voice in my head whispered, *Nah. Forget it.* Best thing that could've happened to me. I thought to myself, *You know what, this is cool.* Whatever. I was hurt, but I wasn't about to let *him* see that. I got up, gave him a hug, and left. No sex, no more words, no nothing.

A couple of years later, he hit me up and I met him in Texas at one of my friend's houses, trying to re-kindle things. Long story short....I found out that he had a girlfriend, and I wasn't with it. After all that time of putting me on standby, he finally decided to give that title to someone else. Not only that, but he was still trying to keep me on the side... smh.

Of course, he was like, "It's not even that big a deal." Man... fuck all that. I'm not about to go through that anymore. I'm not going to get myself heartbro-ken because, in my mind, *I was in love with him.* And I thought he felt the same way... but he didn't. I had fed into the lies for so long that I finally had to put my foot down and say enough. Even though I was *happy* with the lies because I was happy with the way he made me feel...I knew that wasn't what I wanted. I'm not chasing any dude for the rest of my fucking life. No matter how good the dick is. No matter how much they rock your fucking world... nobody should ever have that type of power over you.

***

The biggest lesson I learned from this is that even the sweetest lies can cut just as deep as the harshest losses. No matter how much you *think* you're in love with somebody, if somebody is not 100% free... you move on. Get out of there and get the person who's made for you. There's other people that will give you the 100% commitment that you're trying to give out. Stop settling <3

And I Believed Him

Marissa Sorrentino

"You and Nick would look so cute together." That was what my coworkers cooed at me. There was only one problem. He was married, so I never considered him an option. Not until the day he walked into our office with less energy than normal. "What's wrong?" I asked, genuinely concerned.

"Yeah, what's going on?" piggybacked my coworker, Doris.

Nick just shook his head. He was standoffish at first, like he didn't want to tell us why he was sad. It made sense, I mean I hadn't really known him for nearly as long as my other coworkers had. It must have been something personal, and I didn't want to pry.

Doris slid her chair over to me a few days later and whispered, "Wanna know why Nick's been so different lately?"

I nodded, of course I wanted to know.

"Well, it turns out his wife is abusive, and he's so unhappy that they're getting a divorce. Papers and all."

And... we believed him. *I* believed him. After all, why shouldn't I?

"You can talk to me if you need to," I offered, when next I saw him. "I'll listen, even though I haven't known you as long as everyone else."

He didn't say thank you or anything. He smiled and hugged me. The kind of tight hug that held my chest to his for just *slightly* longer than normal. Not enough to question motive, but just enough to think it was odd.

A couple of days later, he came in whining that he missed cuddling with someone, saying that he missed human touch. I didn't really think much of it. I didn't see it as him trying to hit on me. I'm fat, have acne, and a smart mouth. I've always considered myself one of the undesirables. There was no way I had a chance. Nick was tall with broad shoulders and the kind of charismatic personality that everyone loved. I mean, really, I had literally never heard anything bad about him.

The next day I was sitting next to my coworker sorting papers and laughing and Nick came in saying that he'd been asking all of his friends to hang out. My coworker said he was a busy guy and had to work at his other job so he couldn't hang out but Nick, always confident, replied, "That's okay. Marissa and I are hanging out on Tuesday."

Now, I *definitely* don't remember asking to hang out with him. I won't even tell a waiter when my order is wrong let alone ask someone like *him* out. Now, I may have anxiety, but I'm not stupid. He didn't ask if I wanted to go out. Noooo. He just said that *we* were going out. Come to think about it, he didn't really give me any room to reject him. You see the issue, right? But I was all smitten and had been brainwashed by society to think that because I was fat I should just be happy that anyone at all had an interest in me. Looking back on it, I really should have sensed something was off. I mean damn. I'm studying Sociology. I ought to be able to read people and situations better.

I was so naive. I think in the back of my mind, I *knew* something was wrong. In the days leading up to our "date," I followed him on Instagram, you know, because we could be considered friends at this point. When I went to show my sister who it was I was going out with, I couldn't find his profile. I had literally followed him like the day beforehand. This really should have been the only red flag it took. I'm sure you guys can figure out why I couldn't find his profile. He blocked me! We had a date planned on Tuesday, and he blocked me. I know damn well he didn't delete his Insta because while we were on that date, he was scrolling through it! When I asked him why I couldn't find his profile, he had the audacity to say, "Huh, that's weird." All without eye contact. And I believed him. Didn't even end the date after that comment. Looking back on it, I wish someone had just been there to tell me I was worth more than the scraps he was giving me.

We walked around a park for a little while. He held my hand and my heart fluttered despite my brain rolling its eyes. I actually spent some time just looking at his hands. They were calloused and big and felt wonderful to hold and be held by. While we were out, he got a call from who I thought was already his ex-wife. The phone call seemed to upset him, and he said it was about finalizing the divorce papers. So... he *wasn't* divorced yet. I was on a date with a married man. He knew that bothered me, so he did his best to explain that he really was in the process of separating... and I believed him.

Later, he said he wanted to take me somewhere pretty to watch the stars. I suppose part of me knew what his intentions were at that point. I mean, what could he possibly want to do in the mountains at night? He said he wanted to look at the stars with me. I was naive, but I wasn't stupid.

He got his, and I got mine. I would be lying if I said it wasn't a good time. After the romp in his car, I felt confident. I felt wanted, and that was all it took for me to ignore all the signs.

Later that week, we were taking our lunch breaks

together and kissing in places we shouldn't have been. He talked about renting a hotel room to "finish what we started" in his car. He invited me on his Disneyland trip that was months in the future. I was ecstatic, which is why it hurt too much to see that his status on Facebook (where he hadn't blocked me) was still in a relationship. I made excuses for him. Then Doris, with a sorry expression, showed me his Snapchat story of him at the amusement park... with his wife. We had only gone on a few dates, but I was so ashamed. God, I really had been played. But I was so desperate to be wanted. I'd spent the majority of my youth thinking no one would ever want to be in a relationship with someone like me, so I ignored all the red flags because being desired was addicting.

That Disney trip he invited me on? Yeah, he took his wife. He even had the nerve to change his profile picture to be a picture of the two of them there. My coworkers showed me and apologized. I suppose they expected me to be torn up. I wasn't. I had been played. I wasn't sad, I was mad. Mad at myself for ignoring all the things that I should have picked up on because he said he liked me, and that made me feel like I was finally worth something. Here I was, really thinking my worth was dependent on whether or not I was wanted by men. God, even saying it now sounds stupid.

Later, I found out that while he was studying in

another state he had cheated on his wife multiple times with multiple different women. Can you believe that?

***

I really thought this player's attention was what gave me worth! Please. Neither he nor any other sleazy dude who just can't keep it in his pants can determine my worth or any other woman's. You are a *person* with wants and needs and interests. Whether or not some man wants to date you or mess around with you does not determine your worth. You have worth before, after, and while being with a man. Your worth is your own, not something that someone gives to you. It is intrinsic. And I wish someone had told me this earlier so I didn't have to feel like a fool with rose-colored glasses. I don't need a man to prove what I already am, and that's fantastic! But maybe it's not all bad. I'm glad I experienced this, so I won't settle for someone like him again.

The Guilt Trip King

Caitlin Long

Daniel Lang took care of me ever since I was little. The reason for this is because he is my father. Now, some women have trouble with their boyfriends, but my dad has taken me on a roller coaster of emotions since I was 8 years old. You may think that I am exaggerating, but I am actually not. My father has emotionally abused me for years. The thing that sucks is that he doesn't realize that what he is doing is wrong.

My dad would constantly tell me things like, "This is your fault" and "I blame you for this happening." This would cause me to get very upset and cry in my room. He would also yell in my face. He portrays himself like a malignant narcissist who only cares about himself.

If that wasn't bad enough, he would even find other ways to make my life miserable. Sometimes, my dad would intentionally not pay the water bill, so I would not be able to wash my hands at home or get a shower. This affected not only me but my mother and brothers too. My father just did not give a shit that we did not have basic necessities.

The icing on the top of the cake would be his guilt trips. He always made me feel guilty about something, especially after I moved out of my brother's place.

My dad said to me, "Hey, Caity, it wasn't right for you to leave Mark high and dry like that. You need to help him clean up your room."

He couldn't be serious, right? Why should I have to clean a room I no longer lived in? This just further proved how much of a selfish person my dad was, though. The guilt trips continued for several months. I never cleaned the room because once I moved out with my boyfriend Jordan, I felt like that was no longer my problem. And you know what? I don't feel guilty about it at all because I don't give a crap about what my dad thinks anymore.

I used to be so worried about what my father thought, or I would get upset when he constantly blamed me for things. Then I met my amazing boyfriend Jordan a few years ago, and I realized that there are great guys out there. Guys that actually care about you and want to make you happy. Men who actually listen to what you have to say and support you through good and bad times.

***

I also had an epiphany that my dad was emotionally abusing me. I didn't realize it back then, but I eventually saw that what my dad was doing to me was not normal. All he ever did was put me down and guilt trip me. He continues to give me guilt trips to this day. Now, I no longer fall into his guilt trip trap. Instead, I just ignore it. I feel so much better today than I did several years ago.

I still talk to my dad sometimes, but I no longer let what he says affect me.

Also, a few years ago, I went to therapy after my dad cheated on my mom. Those sessions helped me see that I wasn't crazy. That I was a normal person who was dealing with a person who didn't care about my feelings. The therapy also allowed me to talk about my feelings and express my emotions, which I had not done before.

The journey to becoming the strong, confident, independent woman that I am today took a really long time. When I first met Jordan, it was hard to open up to him at first. I felt like I could tell him anything, but there was this huge brick wall in my head that was built from my childhood. Slowly, day by day, Jordan helped me tear down that wall. He gave me the strength that I needed to love myself and showed me that keeping secrets and not communicating isn't healthy in a relationship.

My dad messed with my head and my heart. Jordan took the pieces of my heart that were shattered on the floor from my father and put them back together. He also helped me learn how to talk to him freely, without worrying about being yelled at or being accused of something. I am now a warrior who has been to battle and won. I have learned to be a strong, independent woman who does not let any negativity or bullshit ruin her life.

This experience has opened my eyes to know who the real people are that care about me. The person that I can truly trust is the love of my life, Jordan. I started out as a measly caterpillar when I was little, and now I am a beautiful butterfly. If any of you are going through a similar situation like this with your fathers, please love yourself and support yourself. Don't let what he says to you get inside your head. Remember, he ain't worth shit.

Numb, then Relief

Sindy Ramirez

As a 13-year-old, love was a new experience. Well, at least the *concept* of love by someone who was not a part of my family was new. I was taken aback when HE admitted any type of attraction towards me; it was overwhelming.

The affection, the unstable emotional spikes, the loneliness I felt after I was forced to abandon my friends for being "bad influences," the threats I received from his inner circle, the constant fear that I was the problem, and that I would *always* be the problem.... It was a lot to deal with.

At the moment, I felt it was my fault.

Truthfully, I was persuaded by a coarse mind. During the time he occupied space in my life, I knew he believed a man's purpose was to be dominant and aggressive, while a woman's role was to remain obedient and loyal, regardless of the circumstance. In the midst of the drama, when I had no idea how to react to his "love," I cowered in fear and complied. Now that I'm an adult, however, I realize that these "rules" he implicated on me were a sign of toxic masculinity proving a lack of interest in my well-being. The black tar of his so-called affections engulfed me.

The trauma of it all has left me with memory loss, where I can remember only fragments of my lifetime. To this day, I can barely recall whole memories unless I really try and relive the painful moments. Regardless of the effort, I am always left with blurs and missing portions. Nevertheless, I can easily recollect every detail of my story with a guy named... we'll call him John.

John was an okay looking kid, for a 14-year-old that had no sense of style, wore snapbacks, and shuffled for Youtube likes that he never received. I had no clue that he would glance at the quiet girl wearing all black, standing with a small group of friends at a middle school dance in a humid gymnasium, and think, "Let me get at that."

Yet he came up to me, reached for my palms, leaned in, and we had a brief conversation.

"You are a really good dancer," he said coolly.

"Thanks, John," I giggled. "You're not too bad yourself."

"I wasn't dancing."

"Oh... well still. Yeah, okay, bye."

And I have never walked away from an awkward situation so quickly in my life. He even went so far as to go to my friend and ask her to ask me out for him.

I said no.

However, my friend thought it would be a good idea to go against what I had originally said. She said yes on my behalf. He then came up to me and kissed my lips. I felt trapped and uncomfortable. I told myself there was no turning back now. Everyone saw him kiss me, and I couldn't say no any longer.

We started dating. I told myself not to get too close, and I never did. I kept him in the dark; I never really opened up to him. I was afraid of what he would say if I decided to leave.

The relationship from the beginning was not something I wanted to be in. But I gave in to the fantasy that maybe he *could* be something more than a pretentious twat, wanting nothing more than to use me.

Boy, was *I* wrong.

In the time that followed, I was scattered, bent, and broken.

It seemed, at first, that he kind of cared about me. I thought *maybe* this could work. Then he began getting aggressive and bitched about how his exes let him do whatever he wanted to them. I always said no, and he did not like that. *At all.* He began to have random spikes of anger and rage. He would violently clutch my wrists and pull me away from groups of people. He would tell me I was worthless, and eventually even started to slap me.

I was 13.

I was so naive, and I believed him when he told me, "I do it because I care about you." In reality, *I didn't know any better*. I was too young to even fathom the concept that this was not okay. I slowly fell into an abyss where I felt there was no coming back from.

I stopped eating. I would cut my wrists just enough to feel a sense of control. I jumped barefoot on broken glass just to feel *something* on my skin other than his rotten, vile hands. I began to wear baggy sweaters and long sleeves to cover the marks, and I even silenced my own voice. His voice was deafening as he continuously screamed at me, fiercely and ravenously, as if he dreaded the idea of my existence. I realized that I was not okay in this position. His friends began to harass me and told me that if I left, I would regret it. They said I would end up hurt, and I believed them.

A teacher of mine noticed the drain of confidence in my classwork and participation, and he saw how close John was to me. The teacher even thought moving him away from me on the seating chart would help. Apparently, he could sense the negative aura surrounding John, but could never really get what his deal was. That teacher would make funny comments and look at me just to make sure I laughed, to know I wasn't completely gone. I appreciate him to this day. Thank you, Mr. L.

It took a year—one whole goddamned year—for him to finally realize he wasn't going to get what he wanted. He finally left. Years later, he continued to harass me. John would elbow me or shove me as we passed in the halls, but I kept my head held high; I *refused* to put my emotions on display for him to relish. I was not going to allow some boorish brute to have an effect on my mood and growth.

***

The bruises from his strikes that caused me to crumple in pulsing pain and despair have forever scarred my perception of love. However, I will never allow these fears to force me into feeling as if I am less than human or a last resort. I can and *will* get better. I will grow and understand that I am a woman who is still healing and manifesting positivity into her everyday life.

My lesson to you, reader, is please take care of yourself. Never allow another person to hold so much control over you. If you do, you relinquish your mind for them to alter, and no one should have control over your *soul*. One of the toughest but necessary choices I've had to make in my life was to forgive people who didn't ask to be forgiven. If you ever find yourself in a position like the one I described, reach out! I regret not telling my parents and sister the things that were going on in my life, and I apologize to my family for putting them through so much trouble. I was scared and didn't know any better, but I do now.

Speak it to the world: IT WILL GET BETTER.

Him, I, and Broken Promises

Honey Chanel

So I'd known of him from around the way for quite a while, and although we ran in different circles, the town in which we lived wasn't all that big. So, inevitably, we had the occasional run-in. As it was, I was taken by his charm and undeniable confidence even though we had never spoken a word to each other. That all changed one Spring Break in 2002...

I was at a hotel with some of my cousins, and we decided to get in the pool. About 20 minutes into being in the pool, two guys showed up and lo and behold, one of them was HIM! I swear it was like I was in one of those Hallmark/Lifetime movies or something because the way I felt at that very moment after seeing him walk through the pool gates was like I had no breath left in my body. I know, I know... it's so cliché, right? But when it happened, he literally took my breath away.

I don't know if it was his smile that just melted me instantly when he glanced my way or the smell of his cologne which pleasantly overpowered the smell of the chlorine-filled water I was in when he passed by with his friend. Right as they were about to be out of sight, my cousin put me on blast and yelled out, "Aye, my cousin likes you!" Embarrassed much? Of course, but I thank GOD my cousin did that because what happened next was *amazing*; a definite *forever* type of situation. Well, at least I thought so.

We were strictly two people getting to know each other for a couple of months. We became friends and made a promise to each other that no matter what was to happen between us, we would ALWAYS remain loyal and brutally honest friends. That alone meant so much to me, and it just further drove me into certain awe of him... being that loyalty is everything to me.

At the start of the new year, he asked me to be his girlfriend. I was over the moon about it, because I had already made up my young naïve mind that he was the "one." We could talk about any and everything, we would literally stay up on the phone all night with each other, and when we would see each other, it was the best feeling in the world just being in his presence. One night we literally stayed out late just sitting in his car in front of his apartment listening to T-Pain's "Let Me Buy You A Drink" on repeat. That was one of the best nights ever. Please understand, I have NEVER been the shy type, but around HIM I felt that unfamiliar shyness coming out. It was a typical young girl full of butterflies around the boy she liked type of shyness when it was just he and I, but when any of his homeboys were around, for some odd reason, I felt like a child that didn't want to upset her coach in the big game. His homeboys—better yet his brothers (because that's what they are to him)—meant everything to him then and now, so their opinion mattered. Because I knew how much they meant to him, I knew being on any of their bad sides would never fare well for me.

About 9 months into our relationship, he and one of my cousins got into a disagreement outside of my grandmother's house and of course, a few of his homeboys were there, so I didn't take sides. Matter of fact, I desperately tried to pay it no mind. He gave me this look that I'll never forget and without a word, he left. For days, I didn't hear from him. For a long while, I blamed my cousin. When I found out he was in a new relationship, I quickly realized I had been played! When people show you who they are, believe them the first time.

I was absolutely devasted. I would literally stay in my room blasting "You A Lie" repeatedly! My sister got so sick and tired of me, being that her room was right next to mine (my fault sis). Eventually the pain subsided. I never forgot, but I chose to move past it.

Maybe a year later, we linked back up. This time I had every intention on just being friends. After all, we did have that promise we made to each other and despite everything, I wasn't going to go back on my word... even if he had. We would talk on the phone quite a bit. He had a surgery, so I'd go visit him from time to time to make sure everything was ok. We continued to be friends even after both our lives started pulling us in different directions. I can only assume he would be there for me if ever I needed him, just as I would be there for him. My mom always says, "A hard head makes a soft ass!"

Five years flew by just like that, and we found ourselves right back in each other's reach. I was at one of his family member's houses hanging out with some of my cousins and guess who walks in? Yes, HIM. And just like that, it was the night we first met all over again. We were a bit older now and though we hadn't seen each other in a while, it was as if we had been around each other every day of our lives. It was perfect. I swear I felt like it was fate we were just somehow supposed to be.

So, in April of 2007, he and his homeboys were getting ready to go play a basketball game, so we walked into Evans. It's a popular lil corner store in our hometown. The cashier asked us one question as he was ringing us up: "Are you guys an item?" Right then and there, we looked at each other and said, "Yeah." That day in that store *officially* started our 10-year journey. When I was younger, my mom loved to say to us, "You made your bed now

you have to lay in it." How right you were, Mom.
Now I should have known better, but hey. Back
then, I was still trying to give people the benefit of
the doubt. The most ironic part of this whole ordeal is the fact that we remade that previous promise to each other and added in that we would *never*
hurt each other. That was a no brainer to *me*, but I
understood that he had reservations about us trying again because he was worried I would hurt him
like he had hurt me before. Obviously, he didn't
want to jeopardize the friendship we had been re-
building. I thought this was the sweetest thing, so I
agreed. Boy oh boy, what good did that do me.

The first 9 years were some of the best years of
my life, and I know everyone is probably reading
this, awaiting a lil piece about our engagement,
marriage, and kids. Nope. That's not how this story goes. There were no rings and vows exchanged,
but it felt like I was in a marriage; we were *happy*.
In any relationship, there is a rollercoaster of ups
and downs. Those that are totally preventable, and
those where the only thing that can be controlled
is the way you react and how you make it through
together. Going into the 10th year of our relationship, I knew something was off and for a while, I
just did not want to acknowledge it.

As time went on, it seemed like every little thing
I did was a bother, or it aggravated HIM. Little things that we would always do together he

seemed no longer interested in. His phone became his world, and oh my goodness... if I dare asked to use it, there was a *problem*.

Listen, you must understand that he was the love of my life. The man I felt that wholeheartedly that I was supposed to be with. With that being said, these new developments only devastated me. I just felt like I could no longer reach him. Not for lack of trying but because he would not allow me in. That last year of our relationship was rough, but we had been through "rough" before, and together we made it through. This time it was different. I *felt* it, and though I became discouraged, I NEVER gave up. The roughness we could have overcome (as we always had), his loss of faith in us, and failure to communicate with me is what sealed the demise of our relationship.

2017 was the worst year of my life. I lost what I thought was my life partner, my friend, my lover, my person, and one day my husband and father to my kids. While I was praying for us, he was busy pillow talking with someone else divulging my medical issues and God only knows what else. She wasted no time giving him a child after realizing that was something I couldn't do for him in 10 years. I couldn't, but she could! Not even 2 months of being apart, he had already become an expecting father which only further made me feel *a way* as we had been trying forever. At the very moment

I found out he was to be a father, all I could hear was my grandmother yelling, "The life of a nigga!" I am going to be brutally honest. After our break-up, shit got real for me. I felt so lost, alone, and betrayed. Man, I had just lost my forever person, my friend, the person I could be goofy with and knew all my flaws inside and out. I was numb all over. The plan I had for us, our future.... it was just gone!

***

Now that it was just me, I could no longer see my future path. Although I wanted so badly to be petty and had *every* opportunity to be, I refrained. Even though I wasn't in a good place emotionally, my faith is what kept me humble and helped keep me going. I prayed more, went to church more, and I had a banging support system behind me (you know who you are). When I thought I wouldn't recover from that immeasurable hurt, God assured me His plan for me would be far greater than any plan I could ever concoct. All I needed to do was be still, keep my faith, and trust him. At that moment, I knew I had to forgive him. Not for him, but for *me and my peace!*

I can't pretend to know why he chose to do me the way he did, and I won't lie. Every once in a while, I still wonder why he felt he needed to hurt me so. At the end of the day, it didn't have to go down the way it did; I didn't have to lose my friend along with my lover.

Loyalty. Everyone wants it in their lives, but not everyone is *worthy* enough for it. I am far from perfect. Heck, I don't pretend to be. One thing is for sure: I *am* loyal, and I deserve a man that's going to match my loyalty with no exceptions. It was breathtakingly painful to realize that after 10 years (in his mind), I wasn't worth remaining LOYAL to and fighting for, but I'm glad I now know so that I don't miss the king awaiting me that knows and fully appreciates my worth! Loading...

Nigerian Opportunist

Wendy Grayson

I was in love. And at the end of the day, this guy was my side piece trying to make it to the first place. Nigel was his name. He used to question everything that my main man used to do. He was always trying to convince me that he should be the main, and when he finally got the opportunity, he fucked me over. This is the story.

We met at Best Buy, and I was just so fascinated with him because he was from up north, and he had family in London. Nigel had the Meek Mill vibe going on with the accent, and I was attracted to him and his big bright eyes.

So, him and I are conversing, and my main and I parted ways. I was hurt, and honestly Nigel was just a rebound that was there to keep me company. I liked him and all, but I wasn't really in a head space for a deep relationship. But I thought hey, since opportunity presented itself let's just see what happens.

Nigel and I started having unprotected sex, and not too long afterward I go to the doctor because I noticed an odor "down there." I found out I had a bacterial infection, and I'm pissed. I hit him up and the conversation goes something like this:

"Nigel, I need to talk to you."
"Wassup?"
"So... I have a bacterial infection."
"Okay... how you get that?"
"I'm only fucking with you, so I'm asking the same question." Crickets. "Who you been fucking?"
"What you mean?"
"You got to be fucking with somebody because my pussy get like this after fucking you, then you fucking with somebody else."

After some more back and forth, he finally admitted he was having sex with another girl. That should've been my first sign, but I shook it off. We still continued on with no protection. Honestly, I wouldn't have minded having a baby with him. What can I say? I fell in love quick and hard.

I was in love, but I wasn't blind to the fuck shit he would do. Take Valentine's Day for instance. He'll call me the day before and the day after. I'd have to beg him for his time. It was a lot of unnecessary back and forth. He said one thing but acted completely different. One day I was like enough is enough because I'm not that bitch to be playing with. He really drove my emotions up on 10 on a regular.

So, when he came to my city, my mother gave him some words of wisdom. Long story short, she said, "If you're not gonna fuck with my daughter all the way, then get the hell on." Oh, yeah. My mama does not play.

He said he wouldn't do it again, and he wasn't going to play with my feelings. Fast forward....and he's still on his bullshit. It was always an excuse with him. When it came to everything else, he would put in 110%. With me, I was lucky to get 50. But still, I put up with it.

He ends up getting in trouble and has to move back up north. I wanted to be with him, so I started making plans to move up there too. We were going to try to make this thing work and build a life together. He had his music he was working on, and I was just going to figure things out when I came. When I told him I was coming up there, he was thrilled. He said that he'd take care of me and give me some money to get by until I got myself a job.

I was like okay, cool. My cousin and I drive up there so she can drop me off, and I meet up with Nigel. Mind you, I have all my stuff with me. Everything I own was in that car because I was moving up there to be with him. I see Nigel and ask him about the money he promised me so I could go ahead and get the apartment set up. Tell me why this guy hands me a whole $5. What was I supposed to do with that? I did not drive all the way across the country for no man to be giving me $5.

From then on, things got rocky between us. Here we were in a so-called relationship, but he wasn't supporting me the way that he promised he would. I wasn't a priority in his life, and it was clear as day. He was being selfish, and I was starting to feel like I was all the way up there for no reason.

So, you might be wondering why I called him an opportunist? Let me bring it all home for you.

When I came up from my hometown, I had brought all his stuff with me as well. He was supposed to be paying for some of those moving expenses. That never happened. The last straw came when one day he called me saying that someone owed him money and they were going to be sending it to my account. I felt a little uneasy about it, but I trusted him. It was a couple of thousand dollars, and he said that it was all legit and normal.

He drops me off at work that day, and I go on about my business. Well, it comes time for me to get off, and he is nowhere to be found. His phone is going straight to voicemail and everything. I find out that Nigel was locked up. I got a phone call from a detective, and I'm part of a federal investigation for money laundering out the country. It all made sense on why he had been acting that way towards me. *That's* what Nigel had been up. That's why he was giving me half promises and empty words. He was using me and my accounts the entire time, and I didn't even know it. I never heard from him again after that.

***

After all this happened, I prayed. I prayed every day for God to heal my hurt. I also prayed that he would find somebody out there for me. Someone that was truly going to be for *me*. Do you know what happened? My main came back into my life, and a few years later, he became my husband.

What did I learn from all this? Know your worth and stay true to your word, what you believe in, and what you stand for. I knew I was worth more than what Nigel was giving me, and I should have never parted ways with my main in the first place. Don't leave the main for a side, and don't every give anyone the opportunity to use you.

Cinnamon Rolls and Martin Episodes

Maxine Mercury

So, here I am outside the complex on the ground, squatting, wearing all black, leaning next to my so-called boyfriend Omari's car, right? On my soul, I know this probably ain't the right thing to do. I mean, I do still love and care about him.

But my head is screaming, *He needs to be taught a lesson! I want him to feel at least some of the pain that I'm feeling!*

Then here goes my punk-ass heart, talking about some, *Yeah, yeah, I know. But this ain't right. I don't want to make him mad enough to strangle me to death. I got shit to do and see. I should leave while I still have my dignity.*

"B*tch, listen, you either do it or let this nigga continue to play you. He ain't been answering your calls, barely texting you back, he been acting funny, and now he saying his license is suspended, still driving his car, but won't tell you what happened?! GET DAT A**!"

Hesitating, staring at the needle-nose pliers I took

from my auntie's crafting room, I remember our first conversation. The night we formally met.

FLASHBACK

It was at a party during homecoming just last year. And within those 12 months, everything seemed to disintegrate just as fast as the connection had started to flourish.
Jamal, my play brother, already knew Omari. So it was through Jamal that I found out he was interested in me.

Before Omari finally worked up the nerve to say something to me, there was an eerie mental game of cat and mouse happening when we saw each other around campus.

It usually happened when I'd be minding my business, doing me before I'd get a "third eye signal" that something or someone in my vicinity wants my attention...and then we'd lock eyes. I quickly adjusted my gaze elsewhere, ignoring his attempts at telepathic communication. I mean, I wasn't looking for love here. And even though there was nothing particularly special about him on the outside, I was drawn to him.

This longing for closeness with someone else could've stemmed from me residing in a new city for the first time, experiencing a new crowd, all while toiling with personal growing pains. I was at my most vulnerable during this period, but there was something I had to find out about this connection. And I told myself, in secret vows, that whatever the outcome, I would be content in knowing that I gave it a shot.

At the party, I could literally feel Omari's eyes watching me while my friend Dawn and I danced utterly inebriated. We getting our life to Future's song, "Freak H*es," when he and his friend Malcolm make their way over to us.

"You tryna dance?" Omari sidles up behind me.

Like a true gentleman, I thought to my drunk ass. "Yeah, we can dance."

"Be careful with my friend!" Dawn yelled over the blaring music while side-eyeing Omari.

We danced for about 20 minutes before Omari led us over to some dark corner in the party with his arms wrapped around my waist. I was completely unsuspecting that love, or something like it, would find its way to me that night.

It wasn't long before we were basically inseparable. We quickly became an item. Omari was at my place more than he was on his own. In turn, he shared his space with me, amongst other things. We went out on a couple of dates, watched a myriad of *Martin* episodes, and baked so many cinnamon rolls that we gained about ten pounds each. Oh, and the sex was *amazing*. When I tell you, I fell...I *fell*... and hard. I was in love. So much so that I ignored all of my instincts telling me that something wasn't right when I'd catch him sneakily texting in the bathroom with the door closed or napping with his phone face down on his chest. My roommate was not particularly fond of him. And pretty soon, it became painfully clear that Omari and I had begun to spend more time in bed than outside exploring the world together. The connection between us started to feel too comfortable.

And to make matters worse, we still hadn't a clue where the relationship was headed. Naturally, after spending so much of my time with Omari, I became possessive of my man. Not possessive in the way that means having a vice grip on his balls every second of the day. I wanted to feel secure and comfortable in knowing that I could be *vulnerable* with Omari. I wanted to be one of the authoritative voices in his life. I wanted us to be an official couple.

But those thoughts were Jet Li kicked to the side with the realization that we weren't technically in a committed relationship. There were times when Omari would leave my place at night to go chill with one of his homegirls only to come back to me. We bickered about boundaries and lines that should never be crossed out of respect. We were going nowhere fast.

And it was at that moment, I *knew* I'd fucked up. I had to take accountability. Because here I was giving so much of myself with little reciprocity. When I tell you I cooked meals, cleaned the crib, and had sex with him every other night...
I played the role of a housewife with no ring on my finger while he soaked up every bit of the undeserving attention. I know now that the situation was mad, but at that moment, I stuck around because I thought I was in love.

We were binge-watching some series in the living room when I flat-out asked Omari: "Where exactly is this going?"

He responded with some "I'm working on me right now" bullshit. *Bullshit.* Yet, even after having that conversation which got us absolutely nowhere, I stayed. I continued to put up with the insecurity and uncertainty regarding where I stood with him.

Omari moved out of the apartment after the spring semester ended. He told me after settling in that he was staying at his homegirl's crib. She apparently had some internship out of state and offered him her place for the summer. I didn't trust him, of course.

I mean, after being let down, disrespected, and unprioritized, I finally caved. I told myself that enough was enough. It was time to start giving myself the love that I was expecting from Omari's ass.

I cried. I drank an entire bottle of wine. I drove to his friend's house and sat in my car for an hour. All I kept thinking about was how good it would feel to give him a taste of his own medicine.

BACK TO BEGINNING

So, here I am outside the complex, on the ground, squatting, wearing all black, leaning next to my so-called boyfriend's car.

And after the last few seconds of pondering, I used the needle-nose pliers to release the air from both back tires on his Toyota.

***

I now know what I did was wrong. Hell, I knew *then*. But that little devil on my left shoulder got the best of me and what I knew to be right for myself. I don't go around flattening my ex-boyfriend's tires. This wasn't me. That wasn't Maxine's higher self in action. It was the lower vibrational self. I acted out of sheer anger, hurt, and what felt like betrayal.

I had ignored all of my instincts, abandoned my morals, and dispelled my higher self. I learned not to give so much of myself to someone who is not willing and/or able to meet me halfway. Sure, I didn't ask for much outside of basic respect in the relationship. Sometimes, however, your "not too much" can be a lot depending on who you're asking. I told Omari what I did and immediately decided it was time to put more focus into myself. I needed to heal. I needed to give myself more opportunity to grow into the woman that I wanted to become. I needed to let go. I needed to find myself. I needed to love me, first.

Stuck in the Friend Zone

Reyne `Williams

I befriended a guy who I shared all of the same classes with. We were majoring in the same field with him being a year ahead of me. He took me out of my normal and made me laugh genuinely. Now, this man was a complete and utter asshole, but I *liked* him. He was the asshole I needed at that point and time because I just left an awkward, heartbreaking situationship...an entanglement, as I refer to it as.

He and I did a handful of group projects together, which allowed us time to get to know each other. He was brilliant, witty, and arrogant.

Let's call this man Damien.

We spent a lot of time on campus just bullshitting around. We texted frequently and would call each other from time to time. He wasn't a huge fan of outdoor sports but loved Auburn football. We spent countless hours talking, and this continued the rest of my junior year. When he graduated, I even bought him a card with a witty note written inside that he valued.

As I was entering my senior year, Damien and I

kept in touch. He had returned home to north Alabama while I was finishing my last two semesters. We had made multiple plans to see each other, but they always fell through because of the distance. Life went on, and our communication lessened, but there was no ill intent. It was the way of life.

Anyway, I graduated college and was heading into grad school. Damien and my communication increased because I was attending the school whose football team he loved. Me, being the dumbass I was, had bought us some football tickets for the school's biggest rivalry game (of course, I needed reimbursement for how expensive those tickets were). We had planned the whole thing out. He was going to pick me up, we tailgate, and go to the game. Fun, right?

Remember, *this* was a man who I considered to be a good friend. If we were to ever get romantic, that was fine with me. The way he talked made me believe that there was something more between us.

Friday before the big game, I texted him to confirm the time we were meeting. Hours went by, and I got no response. Later that afternoon, he sent me a text telling me that he wasn't going to make it and that something urgent came up. I was upset! How dare he bail on me the day before the game! Luckily, I was able to get rid of the tickets very quickly, but still, though.

Weeks passed, and I hadn't heard from Damien. It's close to Christmas, and I finally receive a phone call from him. He explained that his grandmother had fallen ill, and he was at risk of losing her. I was understanding because I knew how much his grandmother meant to him. We chatted for a long time, and I told him to keep me in the loop and if he needed something, not to hesitate to call. He agreed, and we began our regular text/call cadence.

It was a few days after Christmas, not quite New Years, when I received a phone call from him. It was the middle of the day, which was random for him. I answered immediately, thinking he was calling about his grandmother.

No, it was him calling "to come clean."

He spent about 30 minutes on the phone telling me that he had a fiancee' and didn't want to lead me on any longer. He valued our friendship and felt awful for not being upfront and honest with him. He toiled with this decision for quite some time and thought it was the best moment to inform me of this.

Me, not knowing what to say, thanked him for being honest with me and ended the conversation.

I didn't eat and cried for days. I'm not sure why this one hurt more than the situationship did, but it made my heart burn. I cried almost every hour, and it pained me to breathe—I was this way for 2 solid weeks. It took my hairdresser sitting me in her chair to tell me that I was heartbroken because I had loved him. We weren't involved romantically, we didn't have sexual relations, but it was the fact that he wasn't honest with me and that I had lost my best friend.

***

That was the day I looked at myself in the mirror and knew that I deserved better. I deserved more than what these lame-ass men were offering. My worth wasn't based on how men viewed me but was based on how I viewed myself. I'm a queen and damn it, I deserved to be treated like one! I knew that I wasn't going to be Captain Dumbass any longer. I knew I was going to grow from this and be a stronger woman. I knew that this wasn't the end, but only the beginning. I knew I would overcome and tear down walls...and niggas still won't ever be shit.

The Bitterness of Honey

Zoë Luh

On nights like these, when nights are full of the different shades of grey, I remember last summer. I remember the heartache. Those days of hands being too tight around my throat and my face pressed against the cracked kitchen floor. And I know it isn't his fault. I know those weren't his hands, but he brought memories back out of the shadows. I don't know how to forgive him for leaving me to fight shadows alone. I don't know how to forgive him for leaving promises empty and messages unanswered. On nights like these, I remember curling into myself, crying out for my best friend. I remember there never being an answer. And yet, I want to forgive him. I want to remember the roses, not just an ending of thorns.

Most days, I think I have forgiven him—think I have found peace in memories and knowledge that he is happy. Then there are the nights when I clutch my pillow, hoping it will hold me together. The shaking threatens to tear me apart. Nights go by when I am so angry, the moon turns scarlet. Nights when I would give *anything* to hold him. Nights when the only escape is through words because if I don't let them out, I'll explode.

And then the morning comes. I get out of bed. Wash my face. Brush my hair. See the bruises under my eyes and water-swollen eyelids, and I know I've made it again. Therefore, I will continue. I think of how he held his little brother on his chest at night and sang. I think of our hands, holding each other despite the empty space I know is there. I think of the air filled with grasses, and us laughing as we breathed the stars. I think of how there is more to heartbreak than anger and sadness.

There is also the feeling of a drained heart and emptiness reaching through your veins. There is love in the anger that comes when I think I've forgotten it. There is love in the decision to forgive and forgive again. It is a continuous decision, a continuous care. There is love in the way I see myself and my sorrow. There is love in the way I *love* myself and my sorrow. There is love in the way I continue *choosing* love.

***

My love, I don't know when the pain will end. I still dream about you at night, waking up to your heartbeat on my ear. I think of random things throughout the day and go to text it to someone, but stop when I realize it's really *you* I want to talk to. As the months melt, it isn't less painful. I can ignore the ache more often, but when the pain hits, it hits just as hard as in August. It hits just as hard, and

I drink tea steeped in honey to try to drown the bitterness.

Someone told me today that you stopped loving me somewhere along the way. You must have because you don't treat someone you love the way you treated me. I know they're right, but it feels like a language I don't speak. Like there is no translation with the exact meaning. And maybe there isn't, because I don't know a word that holds us in between the blank spaces; there is too much there.

They say you catch more flies with honey. I always learned to make myself just sweet enough to cover men's bitterness. Flies come to me to bury my body in grief; leave it there. I am amber with grief still stuck in my middle. And it's so easy to lose yourself under a man. You lose me again. I heard you don't talk about your little brother anymore. I don't ask why. I'm afraid if I ask, you will open your mouth and spill honey onto memories. Don't let this be you, ladies. Be bigger than the honey that people expect you to be.

Her Last Battle

Bogumila Bubiak

It was supposed to be a wonderful party, like many previous ones. The autumn weather was not optimistic. My pink dress, the prospect of meeting great people—it all made me happy. I smiled as I ran to the club. From afar, I heard the sound of my favorite music. *It's going to be a fantastic evening,* I thought. It was wonderful, but somewhere inside, I felt that something was off. This place, this evening...something bad just seemed like it was bound to happen. My intuition had never felt this feeling before. If only I knew...

"Good evening," said a voice that I wouldn't forget. A mysterious stranger took my hand before I could say a word. I don't know when, but at some point, I just started dancing. For some reason, I still felt uncomfortable, as if an inner voice had told me to run away quickly.

I stepped off the dance floor for a while and looked at the man I had just met, who was staring at the girl dancing next to him. Suddenly, he came to me and asked for my name. It was very loud, so I almost had to shout in his ear. Approaching him, I felt the intense smell of cologne. *Seductive*, I thought.

"I'm Adam," the stranger said smoothly as he asked me for a selfie and my phone number. I felt strangely out of control for some reason. I never gave out my phone number, but it was different this time. There was something curious, intriguing, yet distrustful about this stranger. I saw him watching women, staring at this pretty little girl. Maybe that was his goal? To get her? *Nevermind*, I thought to myself. I felt that I had to run away from him as far as possible. I went to get my coat and saw him standing at the bar. My heart protested, but my mind was stronger. I just left....

I sat on the cliffs, remembering that evening. Many more were spent with him. I stared at my phone, believing that he would call again. Right...

Adam was always busy—involved in many projects, meeting new people, and joining workshops and events. I understood. I *always* understood. I felt like I should support him. You know, give him more space. Busy with my responsibilities, I always put him first. The same man who asked me to dance suddenly became the most important person in my life. Unfortunately, without reciprocity. *He just needs time,* I thought to myself. I tried to excuse him. After all, you can't build anything solid in one week or even one month. You need to work on it... hard.

I'll work for him. I have enough strength for both

of us, for this relationship. My mind was like a battlefield where my indestructible personality, which had won more than one battle in her life, was fighting with my soft, innocent, lovestruck heart. I was ready to sacrifice everything to make his life happy. Adam messaged me that morning and sent one of my favorite romantic pictures. "It would be wonderful to hug you, to feel your presence, before we focus on our work. Yes," he said. "To hold your hand again, to drink a coffee together."

"Let's meet," I said excitedly. "I have a job interview tomorrow. I want to tell you about something fantastic. You'll love it."

"No, I don't have time. I'm busy with work and other stuff. We'll plan something later on."

I called Julia immediately. She was a longtime friend who worked in the same industry as Adam. I wanted to organize a joint meeting and talk about cooperation. I warned Julia that I had not talked to Adam yet and that we would schedule a meeting later.

"Adam?" Julia asked, slightly surprised. "Is this the same...? Milena, I think we need to talk. Today. We have to."

We ended up meeting in the city center. When I got there, Julia looked uneasy. The conversation was short. "I won't help him," she said firmly. Then, in a whisper, she continued. "Be careful. Adam will write to you, seduce you, surround you with his tenderness, give you attention, and leave you halfway, blaming you for too much involvement. He did the same with Ana."

I froze. I didn't believe what I heard. I didn't want to. I *couldn't*. "We're together, Julia. He's a different man."

Julia laughed. "You have never been so naive, Milena. I will put you in contact with several people. Wake up, girl, before it's too late."

It was too late...

Immediately, I called Adam. Adam was furious. He tried everything he could to find out who gave me the information.

"It doesn't matter," I said shakily, terrified by his scream.

"You are a spy," he spat. "Focus on *your* life. Are you going to control what I am doing and what I'm saying? I can do anything and say whatever I want. Leave me if you don't like it. Now!" He hung up right after that.

I wanted to clarify things at all costs, so I messaged Ewa.

> Do you know Adam?

Ewa sent a screenshot of her picture posted on social media two days ago with Adam's comment. "Hello my gorgeous."

> This Adam? Don't worry,
> I'm not his gorgeous.
> It's what he does. Is
> he your friend? So
> expect the same.

> We are probably
> together but I feel
> like we aren't.

> Together with Adam?
> Block him ASAP.
> Otherwise you will be
> in trouble.

Adam didn't call that day. Didn't text either. I felt guilty opening that Pandora's box. I wanted to know the truth. All sorts of memories came to my mind, breaking all trust, hope, and my confidence in our relationship. I remembered Andrew telling me to be careful with Adam. Julia, Ewa, Ana, Elena, Martina, Marianna—the list went on and on.

That day when I asked Adam to go on a trip. He refused. Two days later, when Elena posted a picture from Dubai, he asked for her to "take me with you." "You are so beautiful. Can I join you?" These are things he commented on Marianna's post of her drinking wine at a restaurant. Whatt?!! Adam?!!

I listened to music to forget all the bad memories and started reading new posts.

"Anyone around?" asked Viviana, posting her location.

"Come to my place, we'll chill together," commented "busy" Adam before I checked the location.

"Who else?" I commented to him.

"You are a spy." His words and everything I saw was pure torture. I felt so down. Weeks then months went by. I felt like Cinderella who couldn't wear her beautiful dress or dance with her prince. I tried to talk to Adam many times. I wanted to understand and make him look better in his friend's eyes. "I can say what I want. I can meet who I want. Don't read what I write if you don't like it. It's your problem if you aren't happy with what you see. I'll shout when you make me shout. I'll be angry when you make me angry. It's your fault. Remember, your fault. Your blame game, your love to upset me. It's nothing to understand. I can do what I want. It's nothing to talk about!" Every word was like a sharp knife cutting my heart into tiny pieces, killing me slowly again and again.

I had booked a photoshoot for my new project. The photographer came to take pictures of me and do an interview. I posted the picture with a blue dress and black heels on, happy to be an inspiration and tell my story. Adam didn't react. I phoned him telling him where I was going.

"Wish me luck," I said.

"Ok, go. Don't know why you are doing this but it's your choice."

So much for Adam's "support." His ignorance reminded me where I was on his list. Was I even on the list anymore?

After a while, Adam finally decided to meet. A small coffee shop, my favorite Americano. "It was a great photoshoot," I said.

"I'm sure you focused on checking what I wrote today and to whom instead of your useless photoshoot." His sarcasm was painful.

"Adam, don't treat me this way."

It was like petrol threw into the fire. He became an evil taking me again to his hell. My soul started to talk when my mouth couldn't. The tears from my eyes kept on falling. "I was always there for you, Adam. I forgot about myself to build something new, for us."

He didn't listen. Instead, he spoke his piece. "Who did you speak with?" he demanded. "Tell me now! If you told someone anything wrong about me, I'll fuck up your life. No one will believe you. Do you know who I am? Do you know how many people I know? Be careful. I'll listen. I'll ask questions now." "Adam, let's talk. Listen to me. I'm really down. Talk to me."

"It's your problem. I don't have time to listen to your shit. You have many friends. Go to them. Don't try to blame me for anything, or I'll find you." I went home and felt like the whole world had failed me. For the first time, I realized how bad it is to truly love someone. So many years trying to deal with his destructive personality, never wanted, never accepted. The fantastic times we spent together were like single islands on a shoreless ocean full of tears and hurtful words. But those islands could be a hope, a life, a future. I believed they could build more islands, to cover the whole ocean. To be strong together. To be an inspiration. I tried. Believed. Failed.

Maybe in the next lifetime, under different names, but with the same souls, we will unite again. It's what you promised, I thought, sitting on the edge of the cliffs, looking at the sun disappearing below the horizon. Alone, scared, too weak to get up, addicted to the fight, lost, empty, emotionally exhausted.

"Be happy, Adam," I said, looking at our selfie for the last time. "Maybe in the next lifetime.

***

Love...can bring happiness or destroy your life forever. You will give him your strength, attention, understanding, time, and even yourself. In turn, he may very well give the same to another woman or himself, killing you slowly, day by day, making you feel like the worse creature in the world. Finally, you will start to believe he is right. You will forget about yourself. You will stop listening to people who will want to save you. And you'll keep saying..,it's fine. I love him, I need to be there for him and wait for him.

I went through this. I forgot about myself, my life, and who I am. I started to believe there is nothing that I can offer. I died alive. I felt empty and useless. In time, it got better. Be strong enough to move on before he will destroy you. Don't forget about yourself. Don't!

The Good, The Bad, The Toxic

Olivia H.

Oh, Facebook. Why must you be the start of such an unpleasant experience? You know what...even I can't blame Facebook for the fuckery that ended up transpiring between me and this guy. So...it all started when this guy named Dylan messaged me. I asked one of my college friends about him, and she said that he was a good dude. Valentine's Day is around the corner, and he asked me if I would go out on a date with him to celebrate. I'm like, "Sure!" This happened in our very first conversation. I thought, *Hey this may be promising.*

I met him at one of the sketchiest Walmarts known to the area. He pulls up in this little red car, and I can see his dimples from the window. As soon as he steps out of the car, I check him out. He is tall, lean, and them dimples just fire up even more. When I get out of my car, he looks me up and down real quick.

"You're a lot shorter than I thought you were," he chuckled.

"That's okay. You're a lot taller than I thought you were going to be," I winked.

"So, we have a change of plans," *Ahh shit,* I thought. "We won't go out to eat," he continued. "My brother is in town and wants to cook us dinner if you wouldn't mind coming over to my apartment."

"Sure. I'll go over there!" Not what I had expected but this could be fun. He seems nice, so why not?

So, I go and meet his older brother and soon-to-be wife. We have a lovely dinner... lovely time. Right before I leave, he says, "You know, if you'd like to hang out again, we can definitely do that."

I had such a good time, I figured why not. He was so polite, and his family was too. He was cute.... Deep down, I really wanted to fuck right then and there, but that was just not my way of doing things. I go back to my dorm and smile to myself knowing that my new crush was a sweetheart and a charmer.

The next day, can you believe that this man hit me up at 7 a.m. with this text:

```
I don't know what
you're doing today.
But would you like to go
somewhere?
```

```
                          Sure.
```

Now, personally, I was a bit surprised. I know he told me he was going to hit me up, but I didn't think it was actually going to happen. I was super excited that he was really trying to make an effort with me. We go to a nearby park and just kind of sat and talked about who we were and what we stood for... yada, yada, yada. Really cute stuff. He asked me later if I'd like to come over and watch a movie. We actually went and watched the movie. Nothing funny. Just laughs and good vibes.

Day Three: he invites me back over and nobody's at his house. We're watching the movie, but this time... He seemed nervous but more focused on me. It all started with his long, strong arm wrapping around me and then... fireworks. I promise you, I have *never* been rocked that hard in my life. I knew as soon as it happened, it was over with it. Girl, this man was *legend-fucking-dary* in every aspect. Them dimples contained a demon spirit because as soon as he opened his mouth down there, my whole soul left my fucking body.

When I saw "it", I didn't realize that a male's anatomy could look like that. It just didn't stop going. It kept going longer and longer and thicker and thicker. I was like, *this is going to hurt*. And it did. And I liked it. And it was wonderful. And for an entire week, him and I were literally stuck together. I didn't even contact my roommates. I stayed there with him the *whole* fucking week. I had class...it got skipped. He had class...it got skipped too. I was getting dicked down, so I saw no reason to leave. This is how intense it was.

Somewhere in that session, he did ask me to be his girlfriend. I believe it was right after that first time. So we are "officially" dating. Second weekend into this relationship and he asks me to meet his mom. I'm thinking, *Oh, shit that was fast.* But I really liked the energy he was throwing my way. We were even getting it in while he was driving because I'm petite and can fit into small crevices. We were fucking all the time, and this continued for several months.

Suddenly...shit hit the fan. I did some snooping and discovered he was still fucking around with his exes. He had multiple girls that he was fucking around with. And, of course, I go get myself checked for all STDs. Luckily, nothing came up.

The relationship lasted seven months, just going back and forth with me trying to understand why he was messing around with other chicks. What made me change my mind about him was the one day I confronted him about a girl that he was texting. Instead of admitting he was wrong, he got loud and *ugly* with it. He never put his hands on me, but something clicked like a light switch came on. I started thinking...*Fuck this*. Why would I stay in a relationship like this? If I can go find it somewhere else?

What really put the nail in the coffin was what one of his friends said to me. "Anybody that stays in a relationship like this, likes it." That got me to evaluate my own life. I *don't* like this. I don't like snooping. I don't like arguing. I just want to have great sex with somebody and be chill. What I had with Dylan...that just wasn't it. The toxic traits were present, and I let the sex cloud my judgment. So...I ended it.

Two years later, I actually got back with an ex I should've never gotten back with. I'm working at a bar and in pops Dylan. My heart skips a beat. Damn...I guess I truly loved him. Of course, I try to hide but he sees me anyway. He comes by me and gives me the sob story. Blah, blah blah. He takes me out on a platonic dinner, and we started hanging out for another month. He and I are rekindling our relationship, his mom is texting me nonstop saying how much she misses me, and I'm just an emotional mess. In my head, I'm thinking...*this is where I belong*. He truly makes me happy. So, what do I do? Break up with my ex to have another shot at happiness with Dylan.

We move in together in his hometown and for two months, it was pure bliss. Then...the sneaky shit started again. This went on for several months. I ignored it. I had convinced myself that he's going to change this time. The day before his birthday, he asked me if he can go out with his friends. I said sure, no problem. He got back late and slept on the couch. I thought that was weird. So, I do what I do best. Just call me Snoopy. I snuck into his phone and checked the messages. Look at what I read via text:

```
You know what I can do
for you, baby?
```

I'm...pissed. And I needed to let off some steam. So, I called her. The girl answers, and I go clean off on her then hang up. Meanwhile, he's still knocked out on the couch. I walk up to him and slam the phone in his face. He wakes up looking like he just saw a ghost.

"Who is she, Dylan?!"
"What the fuck are you talking about, Olivia?" Was he really going to play with me right now?
"I'm going to ask you one more time. Who the fuck is she?"
"I don't know."

I lost it. I punched him dead in his jaw, right off the couch. To this day, it was the best hit of my life. The greatest feeling. When I realized what I'd done...I finally had to face facts. What I just did... is toxic. *This* is toxic, and I had to get out of there. I called my parents and they helped me move out that same day. I was going to marry this man at one point...and I walked away for good.

***

The crazy thing about Dylan was that he truly made me happy. We went on adventures and all kinds of stuff, but he was just a whore. A whore that had no fucking standards. He would fuck a couch if it looked at him a certain type of way because it had curves. But this isn't about him...I'm not trying to bash him like that. It's about *me*. It's about us as women ignoring signs early on.

If your intuition tells you that something is not right, and you have valid reasons to think that somebody acts some type of way.... snoop. Don't worry about what anybody else has to say. Snoop and find out. There's people who are going to say that this is wrong...but I disagree. It's called research. Just like you research a paper before writing it, research and get your facts together before you go blow up on someone. Always research and find out what's going on before you make conclusions.

On top of that, if you discover you're researching, aka snooping a lot, then you really need to assess the relationship. Is this truly healthy? Or is this toxic? Think about it and make the best decision for you.

Last thing, and this is super important, if you feel that you're going to hit somebody or want to hit somebody, *leave*. It's toxic and it will continue to be toxic. No matter how good it seems, just let it go. Move on. There's always somebody out there that's going to love you and appreciate you more than a toxic person ever will.

You're Not Like Other Girls

Kat Shelby

Vance and I had a mutual connection from the beginning. His father founded and left behind what is still a booming business in my small town. His father was close to my mother. She recounted their time together before and after he passed—movie nights at the drive-in, pranks in high school, you know...the whole nine yards. There was a celebration of his life when I was ten that ended with fireworks by the town wharf. I was too young to understand the juxtaposed pairing of funerals and fireworks and how it could dull the pain of mourning, yet put the loss in perspective.

Five years later, Vance and I attended the same high school as our parents. I messaged him, "You working tonight?" when my family decided to go out to eat. He washed dishes at that restaurant in town, the one with the display case up front, with all the cakes and pastries, and a cozy bar in the back that stayed open late.

"Not tonight," he had messaged back. "Let me know how the food is. I'll bitch out the cook if it's bad."

Once, he waited with me outside the school for my mother to pick me up. Later, he sought my advice when his girlfriend proposed friends with benefits (I told him it never works). Over the years, he would tag me in memes I liked, stand up for me in a bullying incident, and offer to take my then-boyfriend and I out to the movies to "third wheel it." I brushed off what I presumed were flirtatious comments, offers for just him and I to go out. "I have a boyfriend," I would say.

We stayed in touch while I started college. My third semester was stressful: I directed, produced, filmed, cut, and wrote a film, on top of teaching myself FinalCutPro and my other classes. I was putting my then-boyfriend off, telling him I needed another night to edit. Some nights I was just too exhausted; chronic illness and stress valid excuses but not enough to soothe his consistent disappointment in me. Two months later, I would discover he was seeing someone else. I told Vance this.

One night, after a discussion about current events in the world, Vance messaged, "You're not like other girls. Were I to talk to anyone else about this, it would go over her head." I wasn't like the rest. I was special. I was unique. Informed. Accomplished. Prettier, even.

Wiser... truth is... I couldn't have been further from it.

Just as my self-esteem hit rock-bottom, here was a single man, singing my praises, dangling amorous possibilities and approval before me when I thought I had lost it all. Complimenting one woman while single-handedly taking down the rest of my gender.

Who was I, back then, to say no?

At first, it was small things. When I slipped on black ice in a parking lot and fell, Vance kept walking ahead of me. He would get blackout drunk and text me cryptic messages. I shrugged it off. Maybe he hadn't seen me fall. Maybe he really didn't remember those messages.

He'd add random people on Facebook he didn't know and add them to groups, and brag about the nudes he'd receive from those accounts. My heart would jump at this. I finally asked him where we were headed together if he was on intimate terms with strangers. He got angry, turned the tables, and accused me of not being a trustworthy girlfriend.

"Now look what you've done," he had said and would say. "You've hurt me so much. I'm crying right now."

The somersault feeling in my chest would sink further, down, down, down into my stomach. This happened often. I'd obsess over the details of the last 24 hours to figure out what it was I'd done this time. I'd apologize and console him. Am I really this horrible of a partner? I would think. Euphoria would follow these episodes. It was like a reward after the finish line, one ordeal after another, with the guaranteed consolation prize of the second chance from the person I loved the most. That return to normalcy felt so freeing.

Vance lived a couple hours away and would visit me on the weekends, staying at his childhood home in the next town over. We'd chill in his old bedroom, especially after dinners with his mom. One evening, we had lost track of time. The cordless in his room rang, and he looked at the caller ID. When he noticed my looking over, he told me it was "probably telemarketers." At night? I thought.

I had checked my phone—missed calls and texts from my mom. I panicked, which triggered his anger again, along with my mother's very existence. He ranted about privacy, independence, and narcissism.

"One day," he had said, "you will move away, and I won't have to deal with this bitch again. She will wonder why I never let you speak to her ever, ever again."

"Please stop," I sobbed. My mom was, is, and always has been my rock, my best friend. She was the first person he attempted to restrict from me, and she wouldn't be the last. It would be months before my relationship with her would be repaired.

He kept an assault rifle in the rear passenger's seat and two pistols in his coat with magazines in its pockets. When he visited my family, he draped his coat on the living room couch. I recall the shock on my father's face from the weight when he picked it up. That was that evening of the day we explored the abandoned Coast Guard base. The snow fell in delicate, drifting cascades. Flakes rested on my sweater. In what was meant to be a romantic gesture, he draped the coat over my shoulders, which ached the next day. He had searched for a point of entry all over that building in needless haste, just like he did with everything.

We got in his truck to leave, and we met another on the drive home. He believed it was following us. He panicked, reaching for the rifle, its safety on, his other hand on the wheel. The barrel hit my head.

"I don't know these guys," he had said, oblivious or ignoring he had hit me. He leaned the rifle against his chest as he drove. I sensed his escalating dread and remained silent for the rest of the drive—my foot on top of my other foot, to make room for the sharp branch that he kept by the stick shift and measured half my height. He set the rifle aside when we reached the highway. We never saw that truck again.

One night, we relaxed in my bedroom, watching movies. I struggle to remember which one, let alone this evening in particular.

He grasped his hand around my neck, pushing on my windpipe. I recall both of my hands on his, trying to pry his grip off my neck and failing. A sharp chill spread up my neck, my jaw, my face, and my forehead until the world faded to black. I don't know how long I was unconscious, but I remember feeling a wave of defeat as I fought. If this was it for me, maybe I deserved it.

When I woke up, the TV was still on. Vance was sitting on my bed, scrolling on his phone.

***

Those nineteen years of my life had culminated into a climax—an abusive relationship with someone who made me believe that I deserved this treatment. That I deserved to be separated from my family and friends. That I deserved to have my work and creative life suffer. That I deserved to experience physical, mental, and emotional harm. That I deserved to die. But I survived that night for a reason.

When others come forward about the abuse they suffered, these questions often follow: "If they treated you so badly, why did you stay?" "Why didn't you stop them when they tried to kill you?" "Couldn't you have told somebody?" There is a valid response to all of these invalid, victim-blaming queries—often, the abuser has such a firm grasp on their victim, that the victim truly believes that they deserve this treatment. This belief isolates the victim from the truth: that there is a better life than this, and they deserve it.

I look back, and I was, truly, in love—only with the man I thought he was. That friend I knew for years when he never existed. And, desperate to get him back, I stayed—hoping, somehow, somewhere along the way, he would return. He didn't. I saw hints of that person sometimes in a kiss or a hug. Those small moments were like treats, and I always wanted more. That says so much about the loneliness I had at the time, which I recognized when I was given a chance to heal when it was all over. Survival was a second chance, but that healing changed me, letting me recognize that I mattered.

Filling That Void

Rebecca Boyken

My mom had always been there for my two brothers and me. She was always that kind of person who just knew when something was wrong with us. Half the time, I did not even need to reach out to her. She always had that intuition when I needed to talk to get something off my chest.

My dad was never like that. Don't get me wrong, he was supportive when he needed to be. It's just the touchy-feely shit was not really his thing. He was more about giving life advice for my professional career, financials, and overall planning.

Suddenly, about six years ago, my mom died. It was tragic. Absolutely tragic. Out of the blue, my brothers and I had lost our support. . .our person.

We had to find our own ways to cope with the crap life would throw at us. Our dad was smart, but he couldn't instinctively be the emotional support we needed.

One brother turned to the bottle. He always seemed to have a good time, but I very rarely ever saw him without some form of alcoholic beverage in his hand. My uncle thought the other brother would go the same way or turn over to harder stuff.

Based on his comments to me when our grandmother died this past Fall, I thought he would not go that route. He mentioned that it happened at the best possible time for him while he was in school, so he would have been free to go anywhere and everywhere once he was done. I feel that may have been why he began to focus more on his studies to become an engineer. He would be making seven figures a year, but that was it.

Me? I was fine. Totally fine. That was what I always said. Fine. Totally fine. But, there was something missing. I never really knew what, but I could feel it.

In recent years, I got a couple of dating apps to potentially try to meet a guy or two. I am naturally more reserved and shy, and I work odd hours and days. My crazy schedule makes going out in a rural area in the middle of Timbuktu nearly impossible.

There came one guy, Manuel, who was the first to really stick out to me. He was not from Iowa. Actually, he was from Kansas and grew up in the American Southwest. The only reason he was in the area, which was about an hour away, was for both school and work. Manuel taught seventh-grade science and was in grad school at Iowa State University.

We talked for a few days before I was able to have a free weekend to see him and hang out.

That was a great weekend. Well, at least I thought it was. He was smart and kind of awkward and nerdy. I wanted to spend more time with him and to be able to talk and get to know him better.

The next weekend I had free, I went back over to his place, so we could hang out some more. There was one moment when he was on his phone, checking on a couple of things before we went to bed. I recognized an all too familiar app flash across his screen:
Tinder. He was chatting up with some other girls on Tinder when he had me over.

It should have been a red flag. My friends, once I told them what had happened, wanted me to run far away from him. I wanted to stay. It did not matter. Not to me. It was a misunderstanding. It was fine. Totally fine. I was fine. Totally fine.

Eventually, I followed their advice, and I started talking to other guys. Their reasoning was that there had to be someone out there who was so much better in comparison to Manuel.

And...that was how I had met Adrian.

He was from the area—born and raised. He owned

his own business and loved to disc golf. We talked for about a week, and we were able to go out to dinner together on a rare Friday night that I had free from both my full-time and part-time jobs.

We met each other at the one Mexican restaurant in town, which happened to be my favorite place, so I was comfortable enough to be me. That allowed for us to be able to get to know each other a little bit better and read each other a bit more. Mostly, it was to decide if we would meet again after that one date.

After our dinner together, we were leaving the place, and he suggested we could go to his favorite bar in town. I was fine with that and climbed in the van with him to go to the bar.

We were able to talk some more, and I was comfortable enough (drunk) to start flirting with him a little bit. He was able to pick up on that pretty quickly. He suggested we head back over to his place, so I could see his adorable beagle.

That was the start of me spending A LOT of time with him. I would always find some kind of excuse to spend time at his place and with him. And, he was fine with it.

A couple weeks later on Black Friday, we were talking late one night, and I asked him the one question that I had been wanting to ask for a long time: could we be boyfriend and girlfriend. Luckily, he wanted the same thing. It was at that moment when everything had seemed so right. For once, nothing was missing.

Three months had passed, which gave me more of an opportunity to get to know him better. There were some moments where I was not sure why he would say what he said or have certain world views, and he would mention how he really, really wanted to sell everything he owned and just travel.

I wanted to ignore those things. They did not matter to me. We were fine. Totally fine.

Then, that initial attraction began to wear off, which I began to notice. I could not eat. Could not sleep. Had issues focusing on either job. I even got sick a couple times.

Inevitably, we broke up. There was really nothing more than "I like you as a friend and as a person." We felt more like we were friends more than anything else.

I realized that I was trying to find a guy, any guy, whether it would have been good for me or not, just so I could have a person. When we broke up, that empty feeling grew stronger and stronger. Even though I was living with a good friend from work, I felt like I literally had no one to talk to.

I sought out help to get through those unresolved issues with the death of my mother and just life in general. I was lucky that Adrian was a good guy and that it came to a head now and not later in life. Otherwise, I would be more of a mess and bringing any of my potential children into that same mess.

***

If I could give other women advice, I would say that you need to slow down when you meet someone new. Get to know them a little bit better. Learn about their hopes and dreams, and learn about their values, beliefs, and how they see the world. Learn about what they like to do in their free time. Basically, you need to figure out if you have anything deeper in common besides, "We like the same music!"

There needs to be some amount of common ground between the two of you that would keep things stable once that initial attraction starts to fade. I call it the "Three-Month Rule." Wait three months from the day the two of you start talking before you think about getting into a relationship with them.

Those three months will not only allow you to get to know him better, but it would be the time

that would allow for you to reflect. Why are you
so keen on getting in a relationship with this guy?
Is it because he was really good for you, or do you
hate being alone? Was it a rebound? Are you being
yourself when you are with him? Or are you con-
forming who you are to please him? Knowing him
and yourself better would make it all worth it, and
it would last beyond the few months that it would
have otherwise lasted.

Choosing Happiness

Madison Ainsworth

As a middle child, the thing I have always wanted most is attention. I can't help it. My parents focused more on my siblings than me because I was more self-sufficient than they were, and I learned to be okay with that. So, when Evan decided that I was his focus and I suddenly had someone's complete attention, I jumped. I was in a relationship with Jacob at the time that I fell in love with Evan, but I was unhappy. We were the best of friends, but dating was the most boring thing in the universe. I wanted more than he could give me, so I broke it off with Jacob to focus on Evan.

Now, nobody was as in love with me as Evan. He and I worked together at my first "adult" job, and I was into him almost immediately. He helped me whenever I asked, and he made me laugh when I was stressed or tired. We carved our initials on a wooden post while we were sweating out in the heat for minimum wage, and we kissed in a parking lot after our shifts. We were 17 and it was simple to be together. I know, you're thinking, "Wow, he sounds sweet!" And he was... for a while. I had very low self-esteem, due to years of being bullied about my weight or how ugly I was. People were cruel. So, for someone to finally be interested in me, I thought, *This may be my only chance to ever sleep with someone!*

I lost my virginity to him in the back of his car. Girls are fed the story that losing your virginity is special and sacred, that you should only sleep with someone when you know they're right for you. Now, I don't know about you, but I expected something more magical than the cramped back seat of a two-door car and about fifteen seconds. I started planning our future together nearly the minute after. He slept with me, and to me, that meant we were going to be forever.

Fast forward two months. I was happy enough with the relationship, being fed cheesy lines and sneaking makeouts in his car. But I was also struggling with depression, and all he did was feed into my negativity. I am not sure I had ever felt so low in my life. I spent so much time hoping for a savior in Evan instead of trying to fix myself. It fed into a lot of resentment between us. I wanted him to solve my problems, and he was looking for someone to solve his. The only relationship either of us should've been getting into was therapy, but hindsight is 20/20.

Coming to the realization that you are not as good of a match with someone that you thought you loved is devastating. It makes you question your judgment. I remember trying to cling so hard to the relationship, shoving pieces together where they didn't quite fit in an attempt to keep his attention on me. We were bad for each other. I was so blinded by the thought of losing the most impactful intimate relationship I had ever had that I stopped caring that I was being manipulated. I was lying to my family and my friends to try and defend what I had with Evan.

He guilted me into sex that I did not want to have on his birthday. Later that night, I felt so sick that I had let myself be coerced that when I got home, I attempted to take my own life. My parents forced me into a hospital that night, and I spent the transition into a New Year surrounded by others struggling with their own mental health. I remembered thinking that I didn't belong there because I wasn't crazy. I was just a girl at a low point. After I left the hospital a week later, I went to live with some family for a month so I would not have any contact with Evan. During that time, I knew something was wrong, and as soon as I was back in my own home, I took a pregnancy test. The sex I never wanted to have in the first place had ended up getting me pregnant.

I was still with Evan, even after being hospitalized, but I remembered being so terrified because I knew he would not want me to have a child. I knew almost immediately that I had the world's hardest decision in front of me, and it was my decision alone. Would I let the worst moment of my life dictate the rest of my future?

I decided that I would have this child, and I would make everything work with Evan. If God or the universe or whatever decided it was my time to be pregnant, then we were meant to be together, even if I had to force it.

Listen, if you've ever been in a relationship, regardless of a child or not, know now that you *cannot* force love from someone just because you want it bad enough. That ends with nothing but anger and heartbreak for you, and you're so much better than that. I figured that out, and I left Evan shortly after my child was born when he decided to sexually assault me.

Choosing to be strong and get out of that relationship as soon as possible was the scariest and most freeing decision I have made. I'm thankful I had friends willing to help me through, calling me and giving me the support I needed to pull away in order to become myself again... whoever that was.

***

It's been about four years since then. I have an amazing child who has no memory of her birth father and doesn't seem to care where he is. I have been dreading the day I have to explain why she doesn't have someone else to raise her, but she has never once thought that I wasn't enough. Every day, I get to wake up and choose happiness for both of us. I have raised her with the help of my family and friends because it really does take a village. She is the kindest, most caring child I have ever met, and I get to say, "I did that!" without help from someone who only wanted to hurt me.

Every relationship we go through teaches us something. People come into our lives for a reason, bringing lessons we have to learn.

From Jacob, I learned I needed excitement in a relationship. From Evan, I learned that I could set a standard for how I would let myself be treated by men in the future. I learned that I was stronger than I ever thought possible. I was able to become strong enough to leave something that would've been nothing but pain, in order to make things right for myself and for my future. I've waited patiently and worked on myself, changing my perspective on life from being negative to embracing happiness as it comes in a more positive direction, but not discrediting the hard work I had to put in to make myself a better person.

Things are different now. I'm in a healthy, supportive relationship. I waited four years for it to happen because I knew what I didn't want, and I was not going to let myself settle for less than I deserved.

Forget the danger and excitement, all I needed was someone who chooses me, and us, every day. That's what drives me as an independent woman: my choices. *Choosing* to be happy. *Choosing* to stand up for myself. *Choosing* to learn from my mistakes and never repeat them. *Choosing* not to settle. Nobody can take my choices away from me.

If any of my story feels familiar to you, know this: You are so much better than the things you allow yourself to have when you don't feel like you're enough. You should never settle for anything less than the best. No job, no man, no life is worth your unhappiness. You are a queen. Dust off your crown and stand tall. You have gotten yourself through your worst days, and you have come out stronger every time. Nobody else did that for you. You don't need a man to give you validation, because you are valid, just as you are. I cannot wait to see what you do next, and I hope that you choose your happiness.

Captain Save-a-Scrub

Bianca Scott

"I can give you anything you want and more." Tuh. That was it. That's the lie that had 17-year-old me smitten and completely out of my mind. You'd think being an honor roll student would lend me some common sense. Nah. All it did was make me even more gullible and desperate for the love of a boy. I can say it now because I'm grown, but at the time, I wouldn't dare admit it. I was so wrapped up in thinking I was missing out on something that I had no idea what I was doing to myself. I didn't realize the destructive behavior that I was about to be subjected to for the next 8 months. Damn. And to think it all started on Myspace.

Back when, you know, Myspace was poppin', I got a friend request from a guy who come to find out was only about 20 minutes down the road from me. I'm from the country, so 20 minutes down the road really is a short distance. We message each other back and forth, then finally decide to meet up. His name was Benny. Ladies, listen to me. I was completely head over heels for Benny, and I didn't know why. It was something about him that just made me want to do everything I could to help him. You know that Captain Save-a-Hoe syndrome that men get? Well, I had Captain Save-a-Scrub.

Not being funny, but he really could do nothing for me. No job, no car, and not even a diploma because he was a dropout. Apart from giving me conversation and attention, he didn't have anything else to offer. Well, at least that's how he made it seem.

I shudder just thinking about it. I really allowed my standards to be that low? I really let someone treat me like anything less than the bomb-ass queen that I was? You might be like, but what happened, Bianca? What happened after you all met that was so bad? Sigh. Pour you a cup of tea, sis. Get some popcorn too.

Unfortunately, I allowed this boy to deflower me. He kept pressuring and pressuring me until I finally gave in. Did I regret it? Of course, I did. But I was like okay. Since this happened, he *has* to be my husband. He promised we could get married one day and live happily ever after, so it's going to be okay. Just writing this makes me mad at myself. But 18-year-old me *didn't know*. I was so trusting. I really believed that what he said was true! Wishful thinking. They say that the first person you allow to see you like that is the hardest to get over. There might be some truth to that because... Girl. I was in straight denial about this guy.

I found ways to break into his social media accounts and saw several instances of him dropping the same lines on other females that he dropped on me. The *exact* same lines! When I saw it, my heart cringed a little bit. How could he do this? Did they take it any further than just talking? Has he ever met up with any of these girls? As soon as I got the thoughts, I shoved them out of my head. Nah, this is just a big misunderstanding. It's probably not what you think it is. I know...I know. Oh...it gets worse.

Remember, I told you I was Capt. Save-a-Scrub, right? Well, part of my superpower was trying to help him get a job. I figured if he got a job, he'd be better able to support me. A very rational thought if I say so myself. I tried Old Navy first, cause that's where I worked. Nope, he couldn't pass the test. Thinking quickly, I had a great idea. Who better for him to work with than my dad? After all, I know he's flexible with work hours, and I know that he'd come get him, so him not having transportation wouldn't be an issue.

Chile...tell me why in later messages, he would tell these females that he was going to work with his "homeboy." Excuse me? Your *what*?? I can't lie; I did exchange some words with him about that. Exchanged words, but didn't do anything about it. I mean, it was just flirting and lying, right? Sigh.

I'm parading through his inbox, and I see messages from a girl talking about how much she enjoyed the night before. Another heart stop. When confronted about it, he says that "she took advantage of him when he was drunk and he would never sleep with someone who looked like her." Even though he continued to send her messages after the fact asking for money, I ignored it. I was like, he's probably telling the truth, and he's just using her for money—no need for me to worry.

So...I know you're probably ready to slap the mess outta me by now. Girl, I was in denial, and it was going to take more than that for me to give up on my happily ever after. Besides, I had already invested so much into this—emotionally, physically, and even monetarily. Yep, I bought him new clothes, jewelry, cologne, whatever I saw that I thought he'd like or could use. He was a work in progress, and I was *determined* to make him the man for me. He was just rough around the edges and flirty. No biggie.

Let's fast forward to summer. I'm out in Detroit visiting family, and I get a phone call. I still remember that call like it was yesterday.

"Hello?"

"Yeah, is this Bianca?"

"Uh...yeah. Who this?"

"This is Michelle."

"Okay..." Pause. Michelle was his cousin/best friend's pregnant sister. I never met her, but I knew of her. I had no idea why she felt like she needed to call me out the blue like this.

"Look, I'm calling you because I need you to stop showing up at Benny's house."

*What in the pure f% *!?* "I don't get it..."

"Don't act like you don't know what I'm talking about. I know you still call him and text him trying to get back with him. But y'all aren't together anymore, we are."

Am I being punked? This has got to be a joke. "What do you mean y'all together?"

"He's my man and has been for some time. But tell me this, when the last time you had sex with him?" My ass was still in shock, but I had to see where the heck this was going.

"A few days before I left, why?"

"Because he was just with me the day before that. I'm the one who taught him how to fuck. I'm the one who taught him how to eat. Everything he did to you, he learned from me."

Yooooo?! What the hell is this fuckery? This is his

cousin y'all! COUSIN. I couldn't believe what I was hearing.

"I just have one question," I said hesitantly. "Is he your baby daddy?"

"If you're asking me if he is the one who watered my seed, then yes, he did."

I was speechless.

"One more thing Bianca," she added. "Did you all use protection?"

"No," I admitted.

"WHAT???!!!" she screamed. Girl, tell me why I started to hear her and him arguing in the background. He had been listening in the entire time right next to her! I hung up the phone.

If it's one thing I could not compete with, it's when your "man" is fucking his own cousin. Even gullible ass 18-year-old me knew better. And not just any cousin, but the same cousin who had murdered her own brother a few months earlier. O_o

***

Since that day, I have never spoken to him. Never went near his house, and never even attempted to contact him. I doubt he tried to contact me either. I buried myself into my writing and took some time to re-evaluate what God was showing me. Yep, He got me through that pain. Clearly, this was *not* what He wanted me to bring with me to college.

I learned a considerable amount about what love is and is not from that so-called relationship. For starters, love is mutual. You both have to pour into it if you want to benefit from it. I was giving Benny everything, yet all the while, I had nothing to show for it. Hell, I couldn't even get the respect of being the only woman he was dealing with.

Another thing, I never have to lower my standards to get what I deserved. I'm a humble woman, so I don't ask for much. All I ever want is for anything you don't have...you're making significant efforts to get it. Complacency is dangerous, and a man with ambition is a man that can get along with me.

So I leave you on this note: if you find yourself playing Capt. Save-a-Scrub....stop. He will *want* to match you; you won't have to push him to do it. Respect yourself, and know you're worth it.

Featured Author Bios

*Who is **Bianca Scott?** Oh, just your typical queen who enjoys traveling the world, watching cartoons, spending time with family, stimulating her mind, and listening to trap music. She has a Masters and Bachelors Degree in Communications Studies and loves every single aspect of the discipline.*

Bianca enjoys using her words to touch souls and make people do awesome things. She has been in the industry for over 5 years, and can't wait to see what the future holds.

Instagram: bonka_s

Bogumila Bubiak is an author of many articles in the field of management. She is a flexible thinker, looking for new ideas and inspirations. Additionally, she is also a globetrotter, nature lover, and fascinated by India. A strong woman with a big heart who love people, went through the emotional hell and decided to write her first story.

Many women contacted her telling her their stories, asking for continuing this topic, and requesting support. She decided to say more. What is the next step? Motivated by her family and friends, she decided to write a book. Follow her journey and get more info on her first book here:

Facebook: bubiak.bogumila

Cheryl Humphery pen name known as *C.H Blake* is a Mississippi native, born in Jackson Mississippi. She has been writing since the age of 12. When not writing, she enjoys community service, helping the homeless, and speaking to the youth among many things. Her passion for writing stems from her hope to one day inspire many. A leader by nature, she has had a professional career in food management for 13 years.

*Instagram: iam_humphrey_*
Facebook: C.H. Blake

Devynn E. Craig *is a new author who is currently writing her first novel. Devynn has been a reader and lover of books her entire life. Her inspiration for writing came from her husband, who has always told her he thought she would be a great writer. When she finally took the plunge, she found her passion in writing romance novels. Devynn is a wife and a mother who loves to spend her time outdoors in nature.*

Instagram: devynncraig_author

Heather Wylie is a finance and one-on-one coach and founder of Wunjo Strategies, working with clients to build personalized life strategies. She is the host/creator of Oh My Stars!, a podcast about the curve balls life throws and some tools and techniques to manage them. You can follow her on:

Instagram: @Wunjo_Strategies
Facebook: Wunjo Strategies

Honey Chanel *is a 31-year-old female from a small town about 70 miles S.E. of Orlando, Florida. She is the second youngest of eight siblings, the proud daughter of two military veterans, and the BLESSED woman of a PHENOMENAL family and friends. She graduated high school back in 2007 where she attained her Child Development Associate Credential and went on to attend college in Tallahassee, Florida. She soon transferred to a college in West Palm Beach, Florida and received her A.A. degree shortly thereafter. She is currently a devoted Health Care Professional and is diligently working towards her Nursing Degree. Lastly, she is an author!*

Kat Shelby *is a bisexual, chronically ill writer in Maine. She is currently studying Women's and Gender Studies at the University of Maine at Presque Isle and has a previous Bachelor of Arts in Creative Writing from the University of Maine. In the past, she has worked as an indie publishing editor and marketer. Kat hopes to study creative writing at the graduate level and is finishing her first novel: a coming-of-age, speculative tale. She currently lives with her family and an audacious black cat.*

Instagram: @honeybunnyoligarchy

Maxine Mercury *maintains her status as a Sims™ Goddess, and she enjoys researching holistic methods for emotional and physical healing. She has also received a BA in English from Spelman College in Atlanta, Georgia. Although she loves to contribute fiction writing, she has decided to begin working on a guide focused on improving endometriosis and general women's reproductive health.*

Email: mxnmercury@gmail.com
Instagram: @mxnmercury

Rebecca Boyken has always loved to read, and it was only natural for her to begin to write. Her life experiences have inspired her to read and write creative pieces. She currently works as a manager at a grocery store chain, though she is making moves to leave that job to do something a little bit more challenging. Rebecca attended Luther College and got a BA in business management. She truly believes that she can get people to do what she needs them to do in a friendly manner.

Over the past few years, she has been working towards self-publishing more inspiring stories.

Vanessa Shevat *is an actress, producer, and creator from western New York. She is passionate about animals, traveling, and body positivity. Vanessa spends her spare time creating, reading, and journaling, and is very excited about being part of this book! You can follow her adventures on instagram.*

Instagram: @veechardonnay

Acknowledgments

First, I have to give all the glory to God. This started as just an idea. A thought that led to actually seeing it come to fruition. 20+ women from different parts of the world coming together to create something like this…. it's beautiful. We were able to complete this project in less than 6 months, and I couldn't be more proud. The challenges came and went, but God… God remained constant. I will forever be humbled by all that He has done and continues to do in my life and the ones I love.

To my friends/sisters Jade Smith, Kirsty Douglas, and Tiyana King, thank you for helping me make this project a reality. God knows you each helped me in more ways than one with this. Whether beta reading, proofreading, organizing chapters, or whatever. You all were there. You were my dream team, and I love you so much for that. Thank you for being yourselves.

Darrell Scott, my Creative Director and first friend ever (or maybe arch nemesis haha), thank you for the inspiration for the cover design and answering my billion and one questions about how to make it look right. You also played a huge role in this coming to life. Thanks big brother.

Last but not least, I want to thank my beautiful authors. I can't list them all because most used pen names, but I truly am grateful that you trusted me to take your story and share it with the world. Without you, this would not have been able to happen. God bless you as you continue on your journey as an author and a strong woman.